VOLUME IV

ITALY AT WAR

berg
Plönken
P.
Villach
Auronzo
H
Paluzza
Pieve
Ampezzo
Tolmezza
U
Gemona
Maniago
N
Belluno
Aviano
Cividale
UDINE
Y
Quisea
Vittorio
Pordenono
Codroipo
Solcano
Ternovo
Cormons
GÖRZ
G
Gradisca
Cernica
L
S. Vito
Tagliamento
Palmanova
Doberdo
Ronchi
Isonco
Monfalcone
A
VISO
TRIESTE
Grado
Piave
Pirano
R
VENICE
GULF OF
Y
CHIOGGIA
Parenzo
VENICE
Rovigno
POLA

The King of Italy and the Prince of Wales.

When the Prince was on the Italian front, he asked permission to visit a trench which was being heavily shelled. The King bluntly refused. "I want no historic incidents here," he remarked dryly.

THE WAR ON ALL FRONTS

ITALY AT WAR

AND THE ALLIES IN THE WEST

BY

E. ALEXANDER POWELL

CORRESPONDENT OF THE "NEW YORK WORLD"
AND NOW CAPTAIN IN THE NATIONAL ARMY

ILLUSTRATED

NEW YORK
CHARLES SCRIBNER'S SONS
1919

AN ACKNOWLEDGMENT

FOR the assistance they have given me in the preparation of this book, and for the countless kindnesses they have shown me, I am indebted to many persons in many countries.

His Excellency Count Macchi di Cellere, Italian Ambassador to the United States; Signor Giuseppe Brambilla, Counsellor of Embassy; Signor A. G. Celesia, Secretary of Embassy; his Excellency Thomas Nelson Page, American Ambassador to Italy, and the members of his staff; Signor Tittoni, former Italian Ambassador to France; Signor de Martino, Chef du Cabinet of the Ministry of Foreign Affairs; his Excellency Signor Scialoje, Minister of Education; Professor Andrea Galante, Chief of the Bureau of Propaganda; Colonel Barberiche and Captain Pirelli of the Comando Supremo, and Signor Ugo Ojetti, in charge of works of art in the war zone, all have my grateful thanks for the exceptional facilities afforded me for observation on the Italian front.

His Excellency M. Jusserand, French Ambassador to the United States, General Nivelle, General Gouraud, and General Dubois; Monsieur Henri Ponsot, Chief of the Press Bureau, and Professor Georges Chinard, Chief of the Bureau of Propaganda of the Ministry of Foreign Affairs; Commandant Bunau-Varilla and the Marquis d'Audigné all helped to make this the most interesting and instructive of my many visits to the French front.

To General Jilinsky, commanding the Russian forces in France, and to Colonel Romanoff, his Chief of Staff, I am grateful for the courtesies extended to me while on the Russian front in Champagne.

Lord Northcliffe, who on innumerable occasions has shown himself a friend, Lord Robert Cecil, Minister of Blockade, and Sir Theodore Andrea Cook, Editor of *The Field,* put themselves to much trouble in arranging for my visit to the British front. Nor have I forgotten the kindnesses shown me by Captain C. H. Roberts and Lieutenant

C. S. Fraser, my hosts at General Headquarters.

For the many privileges extended to me during my visit to the Belgian front I take this opportunity of thanking his Excellency Baron de Broqueville, Prime Minister of Belgium; M. Emanuel Havenith, former Belgian Minister to the United States, Lieutenant-General Jacquez, commanding the third division of the Belgian Army; Capitaine-Commandant Vinçotte, and Capitaine-Commandant Maurice Le Duc of the État-Major.

To Lieutenant-Colonel Spencer Cosby, Corps of Engineers, United States Army, I owe my thanks for much of the technical information contained in Chapter V, as he generously placed at my disposal the extremely valuable material which he collected during his three years of service as American Military Attaché in Paris.

James Hazen Hyde, Esq., who accompanied me on my visit to the Italian front, has, by his hospitality and kindness, placed me under obligations which I can never fully repay. I could have had no more charming or cultured travelling companion.

I also wish to acknowledge the information and suggestions I have derived from Sydney Low's admirable book, "Italy in the War"; from R. W. Seton-Watson's "The Balkans, Italy, and the Adriatic"; from V. Gayda's "Modern Austria"; from Dr. E. J. Dillon's "From the Triple to the Quadruple Alliance"; from Pietro Fedele's "Why Italy Is at War," and from E. D. Ushaw's "Railways at the Front."

And, finally, I desire to thank Howard E. Coffin, Esq., of the Advisory Board of the Council of National Defence, for his hospitality on his sea island of Sapeloe, where most of this book was written.

E. ALEXANDER POWELL.

WASHINGTON,
April fifteenth, 1917.

TO

THEIR EXCELLENCIES

COUNT V. MACCHI DI CELLERE, AMBASSADOR OF ITALY,
AND JEAN JULES JUSSERAND, AMBASSADOR OF FRANCE

IN APPRECIATION OF THE MANY
KINDNESSES THEY HAVE SHOWN
ME AND IN ADMIRATION OF THE
TACT, SINCERITY, AND ABILITY
WHICH HAVE WON FOR THEM,
AND FOR THE COUNTRIES THEY
REPRESENT, THE FRIENDSHIP AND
CONFIDENCE OF ALL AMERICANS

CONTENTS

ILLUSTRATIONS

These illustrations are from photographs taken by the Photographic Sections of the Italian, French, British, and Belgian armies and by the author.

ITALY AT WAR

I

THE WAY TO THE WAR

WHEN I told my friends that I was going to the Italian front they smiled disdainfully. "You will only be wasting your time," one of them warned me. "There isn't anything doing there," said another. And when I came back they greeted me with "You didn't see much, did you?" and "What are the Italians doing, anyway?"

If I had time I told them that Italy is holding a front which is longer than the French and British and Belgian fronts combined (trace it out on the map and you will find that it measures more than four hundred and fifty miles); that, alone among the Allies, she is doing most of her fighting on the enemy's soil; that she is fighting an army which was fourth in Europe in numbers, third in quality, and probably second in equipment; that in a single battle she lost more men than fell on both sides at Gettysburg; that she has taken 100,000 prisoners; that, to oppose the Austrian offensive in the Trentino, she mobilized a new army of half a million men, completely equipped it, and moved it to the front, all in seven days; that, were her trench lines carefully ironed out, they would extend as far as from New York to Salt Lake City; that, instead of digging these trenches, she has had to blast most of them from the solid rock; that she has mounted 8-inch guns on ice-ledges nearly two miles above sea-level, in positions to which a skilled mountaineer would find it perilous to climb; that in places the infantry has advanced by driving iron pegs and rings into the perpendicular walls of rock and swarming up the dizzy ladders thus constructed; that many of the positions can be reached only in baskets slung from sagging wires stretched across mile-deep chasms; that many of her soldiers are living like arctic explorers, in caverns of ice and snow; that on the sun-scorched floor of the

The *Teleferica.*

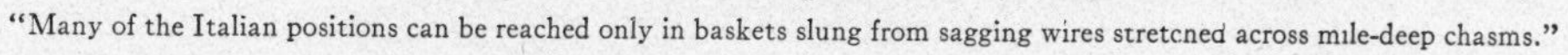

"Many of the Italian positions can be reached only in baskets slung from sagging wires stretched across mile-deep chasms."

An Italian Position in the Carnia.

"Many of the Italian soldiers are living like arctic explorers, in caverns of ice and snow."

Carso the bodies of the dead have frequently been found baked hard and mummified, while in the mountains they have been found stiff, too, but stiff from cold; that in the lowlands of the Isonzo the soldiers have fought in water to their waists, while the water for the armies fighting in the Trentino has had to be brought up from thousands of feet below; and, most important of all, that she has kept engaged some forty Austrian divisions (about 750,000 men) —a force sufficient to have turned the scale in favor of the Central Powers on any of the other fronts. And I have usually added: "After what I have seen over there, I feel like lifting my hat, in respect and admiration, to the next Italian that I see."

It is no exaggeration to say that not one American in a thousand has any adequate conception of what Italy is fighting for, nor any appreciation of the splendid part she is playing in the war. This lack of knowledge, and the consequent lack of interest, is, however, primarily due to the Italians themselves. They are suspicious of foreigners. They are by nature shy. More insular than the French or English, they are only just commencing to realize the political value of our national maxim: "It pays to advertise." Though they want publicity they do not know how to get it. Instead of welcoming neutral correspondents and publicists, they have, until very recently, met them with suspicion and hinderances. What little news is permitted to filter through is coldly official, and is altogether unsuited for American consumption. The Italians are staging one of the most remarkable and inspiring performances that I have seen on any front—a performance of which they have every reason to be proud—but diffidence and conservatism have deterred them from telling the world about it.

To visit Italy in these days is no longer merely a matter of buying a ticket and boarding a train. To comply with the necessary formalities takes the better part of a week. Should you, an American, wish to travel from

Paris to Rome, for example, you must first of all obtain from the American consul-general a special visé for Italy, together with a statement of the day and hour on which you intend to leave Paris, the frontier station at which you will enter Italy, and the cities which you propose visiting. The consul-general will require of you three *carte-de-visite* size photographs. Armed with your viséd passport, you must then present yourself at the Italian Consulate where several suave but very businesslike gentlemen will subject you to a series of extremely searching questions. And you can be perfectly certain that they are in possession of enough information about you to check up your answers. Should it chance that your grandfather's name was Schmidt, or something equally German-sounding, it is all off. The Italians, I repeat, are a suspicious folk, and they are taking no chances. Moreover, unless you are able to convince them of the imperative necessity of your visiting Italy, you do not go. Tourists and sensation seekers are not wanted in Italy in these times; the railways are needed for other purposes. If, however, you succeed in satisfying the board of examiners that you are not likely to be either a menace or a nuisance, a special passport for the journey will be issued you. Three more photographs, please. This passport must then be indorsed at the Prefecture of Police. (*Votre photographie, s'il vous plait.*) Should you neglect to obtain the police visé you will not be permitted to board the train.

Upon reaching the frontier you are ushered before a board composed of officials of the French *Service de Sûrété* and the Italian *Questura* and again subjected to a searching interrogatory. Every piece of luggage in the train is unloaded, opened, and carefully examined. It having been discovered that spies were accustomed to conceal in their compartments any papers which they might be carrying, and retrieving them after the frontier was safely passed, the through trains have now been discontinued, passengers and luggage, after the examination at the frontier, being sent on by another train. In addition to the French and Italian secret-service officials, there are now on duty at the various frontier stations, and likewise in Athens, Naples, and Rome, keen-eyed young officers of the "Hush-Hush Brigade," as the British Intelligence Department is disrespectfully called, whose business it is to scrutinize the thousands of British subjects — officers returning from India, Egypt, or Salonika, or from service with the Mediterranean fleet, King's messengers, diplomatic couriers— who are constantly crossing Italy on their way to or from England.

That the arm of the enemy is very long, and that it is able to strike at astounding distances and in the most unexpected places, is brought sharply home to one as the train pulls out of the Genoa station. From Genoa to Pisa, a distance of a hundred miles, the railway closely hugs the Mediterranean shore. At night all the curtains on that side of the train must be kept closely drawn and, as an additional precaution, the white electric-light bulbs in the corridors and compartments have been replaced by violet ones. If you ask the reason for this you are usually met with evasions. But, if you persist, you learn that it is done to avoid the danger of the trains being shelled by Austrian submarines! (Imagine, if you please, the passengers on the New York-Boston trains being ordered to keep their windows darkened because enemy submarines have been reported off the coast.) In this war remoteness from the firing-line does not assure safety. Spezia, for example, which is a naval base of the first importance, is separated from the firing-line by the width of the Italian peninsula. Until a few months ago its inhabitants felt as snug and safe as though they lived in Spain. Then, one night, an Austrian airman crossed the Alps, winged his way above the Lombard plain, and let loose on Spezia a rain of bombs which caused many deaths and did enormous damage.

Even the casual traveller in Italy to-day cannot fail to be struck by the prosperity which the war has brought to the great manufacturing cities of the north as contrasted with the commercial stagnation which prevails in the southern provinces of the kingdom. In the munition plants, most of which are in the north, are employed upward of half a million workers, of whom 75,000 are women. Genoa, Milan, and Turin are a-boom with industry. The great automobile factories have expanded amazingly in order to meet the demand for shells, field-guns, and motor-trucks. Turin, as an officer smilingly remarked, "now consists of the Fiat factory and a few houses." The United States is not the only country to produce that strange breed known as munitions millionaires. Italy has them also—and the jewellers and champagne agents are doing a bigger business than they have ever done before.

As the train tears southward into Tuscany you begin to catch fleeting glimpses of the men who are making possible this sudden prosperity—the men who are using the motor-trucks and the shells and the field-guns. *They* don't look very prosperous or very happy. Sometimes you see them drawn up on the platforms of wayside stations, shivering beneath their scanty capes in the chill of an Italian dawn. Usually there is a background of wet-eyed women, with shawls drawn over their heads, and nearly always with babies in their arms. And on nearly every siding were standing long trains of box-cars, bedded with straw and filled with these same wiry, brown-faced little men in their rat-gray uniforms, being hurried to the fighting in the north. It reminded me of those long cattle-trains one sees in the Middle West, bound for the Chicago slaughter-houses.

Rome in war-time is about as cheerful as Coney Island in midwinter. Empty are the enticing little shops on the Piazza di Spagna. Gone from the marble steps are the artists' models and the flower-girls. To visit the galleries of the Vatican is to stroll through an echoing marble tomb. The guards and custodians no longer welcome you for the sake of your tips, but for the sake of your company. The King, who is with the army, visits Rome only rarely; the Queen occupies a modest villa in the country; the Palace of the Quirinal has been turned into a hospital. The great ball-room, the state dining-room, the throne-room, even the Queen's sun-parlor, are now filled with white cots, hundreds and hundreds of them, each with its bandaged occupant, while in the famous gardens where Popes and Emperors and Kings have strolled, convalescent soldiers now laze in the sun or on the gravelled paths play at bowls. In giving up their home for the use of the wounded, the King and Queen have done a very generous and noble thing, and the Italian people are not going to forget it.

If Rome, which is the seat of government, shows such unmistakable signs of depression, imagine the stagnation of Florence, which has long been as dependent upon its crop of tourists as a Dakota farmer is upon his crop of wheat. The Cascine Gardens, in the old days one of the gayest promenades in Europe, are as lonely as a cemetery. At those hotels on the Lung' Arno, which remain open, the visitor can make his own terms. The Via Tornabuoni is as quiet as a street in a country town. The dealers in antiques, in souvenirs, in pictures, in marbles, have most of them put up their shutters and disappeared, to return, no doubt, in happier times.

There is in the Via Tornabuoni, midway between Giacosa's and the American Consulate, an excellent barber shop. The owner, who learned his trade in the United States, is the most skilful man with scissors and razor that I know. His customers came from half the countries of the globe.

"But they are all gone now," he told me sadly. "Some are fighting, some have been killed, the others have gone back to their homes until the war is over. Three years ago I had as nice a little business as a man could ask for. To-day I do not make enough to pay my rent. But it doesn't make much difference, for next month my class is called to the colors, and in the spring my son, who will then be eighteen, will also have to go."

No, they're not very enthusiastic over the war in Florence. But you can't blame them, can you?

In none of the great cities known and loved by Americans has the war wrought such startling changes as in Venice. Because it is a naval base of the first importance, because it is almost within sight of the Austrian coast, and therefore within easy striking distance of Trieste, Fiume, and Pola, and because throughout Venetia Austrian spies abound, Venice is a closed city. It reminded me of a beautiful playhouse which had been closed for an indefinite period: the fire-curtain lowered, the linen covers drawn over the seats, the carpets rolled up, the scenery stored away, the great stage empty and desolate. Gone are the lights, the music, the merriment which made Venice one of the happiest and most care free of cities.

Because of the frequent air raids—Venice has been attacked from the sky nearly a hundred times since the war began—the city is put to bed promptly at nightfall. To show a light from a door or window after dark is to invite a domiciliary visit from the police and, quite possibly, arrest on the charge of attempting to communicate with the enemy. The illumination of the streets is confined to small candle-power lights in blue or purple bulbs, the weakened rays being visible for only a short distance. To stroll at night in the darkened streets is to risk falling into a canal, while the use of an electric torch would almost certainly result in arrest as a spy. The ghastly effect produced by the purple lights, the utter blackness of the canals, the deathly silence, broken only by the sound of water lapping the walls of the empty palazzos, combine to give the city a peculiarly weird and sepulchral appearance.

Of the great hotels which line the Canale Grande, only the Danieli remains open. Over the others fly the Red Cross flags, and in their windows and on their terraces lounge wounded soldiers. The smoking-room of the Danieli, where so many generations of travelling Americans have chatted over their coffee and cigars, has been converted into a *rifugio,* in which the guests can find shelter in case of an air attack. A bomb-proof ceiling has been made of two layers of steel rails, laid crosswise, and ramparts of sand-bags have been built against the walls. On the doors of the bedrooms are posted notices urging the guests, when hostile aircraft are reported, to make directly for the *rifugio,* and remain there until the raid is over. In other cities in the war zone the inhabitants take to their cellars during aerial attacks, but in Venice there are no cellars, and the buildings are, for the most part, too old and poorly built to afford safety from bombs. To provide adequate protection for the population, particularly in the poorer and more congested districts of the city, has, therefore, proved a serious problem for the authorities. Owing to its situation, Venice is extremely vulnerable to air attacks, for the Austrian seaplanes, operating from Trieste or Pola, can glide across the Adriatic under cover of darkness, and are over the city before their presence is discovered. Before the anti-aircraft guns can get their range, or the Italian airmen can rise and engage them, they have dropped their bombs and fled. Although, generally speaking, the loss of life resulting from these aerial forays is surprising small, they are occasionally very serious affairs. During an air raid on Padua, which occurred a few days before I was there, a bomb exploded in the midst of a crowd of terrified townspeople who were struggling to gain entrance to a *rifugio.* In that affair 153 men, women, and children lost their lives.

The admiral in command of Venice showed me a map of the city, which, with the exception of a large rectangle, was thickly sprinkled with small red dots. There must have been several hundred of them.

"These dots," he explained, "indicate where Austrian bombs have fallen."

"This part of the city seems to have been peculiarly fortunate," I remarked, placing my finger on the white square.

"That," said he, "is the Arsenal. For obvious reasons we do not reveal whether any bombs have fallen there."

Considering the frequency with which Venice has been attacked from the air, its churches, of which there are an extraordinary number, have escaped with comparatively little damage. Only four, in fact, have suffered seriously. Of these, the church of Santa Maria Formosa has sustained the greatest damage, its magnificent interior, with the celebrated decorations by Palma Vecchio, having been transformed through the agency of an Austrian bomb, into a heap of stone and plaster. Another bomb chose as its target the great dome of the church of San Pietro di Castello, which stands on the island of San Pietro, opposite the Arsenal. On the Grand Canal, close by the railway-station, is the Chiesa degli Scalzi, whose ceiling by Tiepolo, one of the master's greatest works, has suffered irreparable injury. Santi Giovanni e Páolo, next to St. Mark's the most famous church in Venice, has also been shattered by a bomb.

I asked the officer in command of the aerial defenses of Venice if he thought that the Austrian airmen intentionally bomb churches, hospitals, and monuments, as has been so often asserted in the Allied press.

"It's this way," he explained. "A dozen aviators are ordered to bombard a certain city. Three or four of them are real heroes and, at the risk of their lives, descend low enough to make certain of their targets before releasing their bombs. The others, however, rather than come within range of the anti-aircraft guns, remain at a safe height, drop their bombs at random as soon as they are over the city, and then clear out. Is it very surprising, then, that bombs dropped from a height of perhaps ten thousand feet, by aircraft travelling sixty miles an hour, miss the forts and barracks for which they are intended and hit churches and dwellings instead?"

Intentional or not, the bombardment of the Venetian churches is a blunder for which the Austrians will pay dearly in loss of international good-will. A century hence these shattered churches will be pointed out to visitors as the work of the modern Vandals, and lovers of art and beauty throughout the world will execrate the nation which permitted the sacrilege. They have destroyed glass and paintings and sculptures that were a joy to the whole world, they have undone the work of saints and heroes and masters, and they have gained no corresponding military advantage. In every city which has been subjected to air raids the inhabitants have been made more obstinate, more iron-hard in their determination to keep on fighting. The sight of shattered churches, of wrecked dwellings, of mangled women and dead babies, does not terrify or dismay a people: it infuriates them. In the words of

Talleyrand: "It is worse than a crime; it is a mistake."

The strangest sight in Venice to-day is St. Mark's. There is nothing in its present appearance, inside or out, to suggest the famous cathedral which so many millions of people have reverenced and loved. Indeed, there is little about it to suggest a church at all. It looks like a huge and ugly warehouse, like a car barn, like a Billy Sunday tabernacle, for, in order to protect the wonderful mosaics and marbles which adorn the church's western façade, it has been sheathed, from ground to roof, with unpainted planks, and these, in turn, have been covered with great squares of asbestos. By this use of fire-proof material it is hoped that, even should the church be hit by a bomb, there may be averted a fire such as did irreparable damage to the Cathedral of Rheims.

The famous bronze horses have been removed from their place over the main portal of St. Mark's, and taken, I believe, to Florence. It is not the first travelling that they have done, for from the triumphal arch of Nero they once looked down on ancient Rome. Constantine sent them to adorn the imperial hippodrome which he built in Constantinople, whence the Doge Dandolo brought them as spoils of war to Venice when the thirteenth century was still young. In 1797 Napoleon carried them to Paris, but after the downfall of the Emperor they were brought back to Venice by the Austrians and restored to their ancient position. There they remained for just a hundred years, until the menace of the Austrian aircraft necessitated their hasty removal to a place of safety. Of them one of Napoleon's generals is said to have remarked disparagingly: "They are too coarse in the limbs for cavalry use, and too light for the guns." In any event, they were the only four horses, alive or dead, in the whole city, and the Venetians love them as though they were their children.

If in its war dress the exterior of St. Mark's presents a strange appearance, the transformation of the interior is positively startling. Nothing that ingenuity can suggest has been left undone to protect the sculptures, mosaics, glass, and marbles which, brought by the seafaring Venetians from the four corners of the globe, make St. Mark's the most beautiful of churches. Everything portable has been removed to a place of safety, but the famous mosaics, the ancient windows, and the splendid carvings it is impossible to remove, and they are the most precious of all. The two pulpits of colored marbles and the celebrated screen with its carven figures are now hidden beneath pyramids of sand-bags. The spiral columns of translucent alabaster which support the altar, are padded with excelsior and wrapped with canvas. Swinging curtains of quilted burlap protect the walls of the chapels and transepts from flying shell fragments. Yet all these precautions would probably avail but little were a bomb to strike St. Mark's. In the destruction that would almost certainly result there would perish mosaics and sculptures which were in their present places when Vienna was still a Swabian village, and Berlin had yet to be founded on the plain above the Spree.

If it has proved difficult to protect from airplane fire the massive basilica of St. Mark's, consider the problem presented to the authorities by the Palace of the Doges, that creation of fairylike loveliness, whose exquisite façades, with their delicate window tracery and fragile carvings, would be irretrievably ruined by a well-aimed bomb. In order to avert such a disaster, it was proposed to protect the façades of the palace by enclosing the building in temporary walls of masonry. It was found, however, that this plan was not feasible, as the engineers reported that the piles on which the ancient building is poised would submerge if subjected to such an additional weight. All that they have been able to do, therefore, is to shore up the arches of the loggia with beams, fill up the windows with brick and plaster, and pray to the patron saint of Venice to save the city's most exquisite structure.

The gilded figure of an angel, which for so many centuries has looked down on Venice from the summit of the Campanile, has been given a dress of battleship gray that it may not serve as a landmark for the Austrian aviators. Over the celebrated equestrian statue of Colleoni—of which Ruskin said: "I do not believe there is a more glorious work of sculpture existing in the world"—has been erected a titanic armored sentry-box, which is covered, in turn, with layer upon layer of sand-bags. Could the spirit of that great soldier of fortune be consulted, however, I rather fancy that he would insist upon sitting his bronze warhorse, unprotected and unafraid, facing the bombs of the Austrian airmen just as he used to face the bolts of the Austrian crossbowmen.

The commercial life of Venice is virtually at a standstill. Most of the glass and lace manufactories have been forced to shut down. The dealers in curios and antiques lounge idly in their doorways, deeming themselves fortunate if they make a sale a month. All save one or two of the great hotels which have not been taken over by the Government for hospitals have had to close their doors. The hordes of guides and boatmen and waiters who depended for their living upon the tourists are—such of them as have not been called to the colors—without work and in desperate need. In normal times a quarter of Venice's 150,000 inhabitants are paupers, and this percentage must have enormously increased, for, notwithstanding the relief measures which the Government has taken, unemployment is general, the prices of food are constantly increasing, and coal has become almost impossible to obtain. Fishing, which was one of the city's chief industries, is now an exceedingly hazardous employment because of submarines and floating mines. Save for the clumsy craft of commerce, the gondolas have largely disappeared, and with them has disappeared, only temporarily, let us hope, the most picturesque feature of Venetian life. They have been driven off by the slim, polished, cigar-shaped power-boats, which tear madly up and down and crossways of the canals in the service of the military government and of the fleet. To use a gondola, particularly at night, is as dangerous as it would be to drive upon a motor race-course with a horse and buggy, for, as no lights are permitted, one is in constant peril of being run down by the recklessly driven power craft, whose wash, by the way, is seriously affecting the foundations of many of the palazzos.

It is an unfamiliar, gloomy, mysterious place, is war-time Venice, but in certain respects I liked it better than the commercialized city of antebellum days. Gone are the droves of loud-voiced tourists, gone the impudent boatmen, the importunate beggars, the impertinent guides, gone the glare of lights and the blare of cheap music. No longer do the lantern-strung barges of the musicians gather nightly off the Molo. No longer across the waters float the strains of *"Addio di Napoli"* and *"Ciri-Biri-Bi"*; the Canale Grande is dark and silent now. The tourist hostelries, on whose terraces at night gleamed the white shirt-fronts of men and the white shoulders of women, now have as their only guests the white-bandaged wounded. In its darkness, its mystery, its silence, it is once again the Venice of the Middle Ages, the Venice of lovers and conspirators, of inquisitors and assassins, the Venice of which Shakespeare sang.

But with the coming of dawn the Venice of the twelfth century is abruptly transformed into the Venice of the twentieth. The sun, rising out of the Adriatic, turns into ellipsoids of silver the aluminum-colored observation balloons which form the city's first line of aerial defense. As the sun climbs higher it brings into bold relief the lean barrels of the anti-aircraft guns, which, from the roofs of the buildings to the seaward, sweep the eastern sky. Abreast the Public Gardens the great war-ships, in their coats of elephant-gray, swing lazily at their moorings. Near the Punta della Motta lie the destroyers, like greyhounds held in leash. Off the Riva Schiavoni, on the very spot, no doubt, where Dandolo's war-galleys lay, are anchored the British submarines. And atop his granite column, a link with the city's glorious and warlike past, still stands the winged lion of St. Mark, snarling a perpetual challenge at his ancient enemy—Austria.

The Comando Supremo, or Great Headquarters, of the Italian army is at Udine, an ancient Venetian town some twenty miles from the Austrian frontier. This is supposed to be a great secret, and must not be mentioned in letters or newspaper despatches, it being assumed that, were the Austrians to learn of the presence in Udine of the Comando Supremo, their airmen would pay inconvenient visits to the town, and from the clouds would drop their steel calling-cards on the King and General Cadorna. So, though every one in Italy is perfectly aware that the head of the Government and the head of the army are at Udine, the fact is never mentioned in print. To believe that the Austrians are ignorant of the whereabouts of the Italian high command is to severely strain one's credulity. The Italians not only know where the Austrian headquarters is situated, but they know in which houses the various generals live, and the restaurants in which they eat. This extreme reticence of the Italians seems a little irksome and overdone after the frankness one encounters on the French and British fronts, but it is due, no doubt, to the admonitions which are posted in hotels, restaurants, stations, and railway carriages throughout Italy: "It is the patriotic duty of good citizens not to question the military about the war," and : "The military are warned not to discuss the war with civilians. An indiscreet friend can be as dangerous as an enemy."

My previous acquaintance with Udine had been confined to fleeting glimpses of it from the windows of the Vienna-Cannes express. Before the war it was, like the other towns which dot the Venetian plain, a quaint, sleepy, easy-going place, dwelling in the memories of its past, but with the declaration of hostilities it suddenly became one of the busiest and most important places in all Italy. From his desk in the Prefecture, General Cadorna, a short, wiry, quick-moving man in the middle sixties, with a face as hard and brown as a hickory-nut, directs the operations of the armies along that four-hundred-and-fifty-mile-long battle-line which stretches from the Stelvio to the sea. The cobble-paved streets and the vaulted arcades are gay with many uniforms, for, in addition to the hundreds of staff and divisional officers quartered in Udine, the French, British, Russian, and Belgian Governments maintain there military missions, whose business it is to keep the staffs of their respective armies constantly in touch with the Italian high command, thus securing practical co-operation. In a modest villa, a short distance outside the town, dwells the King, who has been on the front almost constantly since the war began. Although, as ruler of the kingdom, he is commander-in-chief of the Italian armies, he rarely gives advice unless it is asked for,

The King of Italy and General Cadorna at Castelnuovo.

Scarcely a day passes that the King does not visit some sector of the battle-line, but he rarely gives advice unless it is asked for, and never interferes with the decisions of the Comando Supremo.

The Peril in the Clouds.

The gunners of an Italian anti-aircraft battery sight an Austrian airplane.

and never interferes with the decisions of the Comando Supremo. Scarcely a day passes that he does not visit some sector of the battle-line. Officers and men in some of the lonely mountain commands told me that the only general who has visited them is the King. Should he venture into exposed positions, as he frequently does, he is halted by the local command. It is, of course, tactfully done. "I am responsible for your Majesty's safety," says the officer. "Were there to be an accident I should be blamed." Whereupon the King promptly withdraws. If he is not permitted to take unnecessary risks himself, neither will he permit others. When the Prince of Wales visited the Italian front last summer, he asked permission to enter a certain first-line trench, which was being heavily shelled. The King bluntly refused. "I want no historic incidents here," he remarked dryly.

To obtain a room in Udine is as difficult as it is to obtain hotel accommodation in New York during the Automobile Show. But, because I was a guest of the Government, I found that a room had been reserved for me by the Comando Supremo at the Hotel Croce di Malta. I was told that since the war three proprietors of this hotel had made their fortunes and retired, and after I received my bill I believed it. There was in my room one of those inhospitable, box-shaped porcelain stoves so common in North Italy and the Tyrol. To keep a modest wood-fire going in that stove cost me exactly thirty lire (about six dollars) a day. But a fire was a necessity. Luxuries came higher. Yet the scene in the hotel's shabby restaurant at the dinner-hour was well worth the fantastic charges, for there gathered there nightly as interesting a company as I have not often seen under one roof: a poet and novelist who has given to Italy the most important literary work since the days of the great classics, and who, by his fiery and impassioned speeches, did more than any single person to force the nation's entrance into the war; an American dental surgeon who abandoned an enormously lucrative practice in Rome to establish at the front a hospital where he has performed feats approaching the magical in rebuilding shrapnel-shattered faces; a Florentine connoisseur, probably the greatest living authority on Italian art, who has been commissioned with the preservation of all the works of art in the war zone; an English countess who is in charge of an X-ray car which operates within range of the Austrian guns; a young Roman noble whom I had last seen, in pink, in the hunting-field, a group of khaki-clad officers from the British mission, cold and aloof of manner despite their being among allies; a party of Russians, their hair clipped to the skull, their green tunics sprinkled with stars and crosses; half a dozen French military attachés in beautifully cut uniforms of horizon-blue; and Italian officers, animated and gesticulative, on whose breasts were medal ribbons showing that they had fought in forgotten wars in forgotten corners of Africa. At one table they were discussing the probable date of some Roman remains which had just been unearthed at Aquileia; at another an argument was in progress over the merits of *vers libre;* one of the Russians was explaining a new system he had evolved for breaking the bank at Monte Carlo; the young English countess was retailing the latest jokes from the London music-halls, but nowhere did I hear mentioned the grim and bloody business which had brought us, of so many minds and from so many lands, to this shabby, smoke-filled, garlic-scented room in this little frontier town. Yet, had the door been opened, and had we stilled our voices, we could have heard, quite plainly, the sullen grumble of the cannon.

II

WHY ITALY WENT TO WAR

TO understand why Italy is at war you have only to look at the map of Central Europe. You can hardly fail to be struck by the curious resemblance which the outline of the Austro-Hungarian Empire bears to a monstrous bird of prey hovering threateningly over Italy. The body of the bird is formed by Hungary; Bohemia is the right wing, Bosnia and Dalmatia constitute the left; the Tyrol represents the head, while the savage beak, with its open jaws, is formed by that portion of the Tyrol commonly known as the Trentino. And that savage beak, you will note, is buried deep in the shoulder of Italy, holding between its jaws, as it were, the Lake of Garda. To continue the simile, it will be seen that the talons of the bird, formed by the Istrian Peninsula, reach out over the Adriatic in threatening proximity to Venice and the other Italian coast towns. It is to end the intolerable menace of that beak and those claws that Italy is fighting. There you have it in a nutshell.

Just as in France, since 1870, the national watchword has been "Alsace-Lorraine," so in

Italy, for upward of half a century, the popular cry has been *"Italia Irredenta"*—Italy Unredeemed. It was a deep and bitter disappointment to all Italians that, upon the formation in 1866 of the present kingdom, there should have been left under Austrian dominion two regions which, in population, in language, and in sentiment, were essentially Italian. These "unredeemed" regions were generally called after their respective capital cities: Trent and Trieste. But, though the phrase *Italia Irredenta* was originally interpreted as referring only to the Trentino and Trieste, it has gradually assumed, in the course of years, a broader significance, until now it includes all that portion of the Tyrol lying south of the Brenner, the Carso plateau, Trieste and its immediate hinterland, the entire Istrian Peninsula, the Hungarian port of Fiume, and the whole of Dalmatia and Albania. In other words, the Irredentists of to-day—and, since Italy entered the war, virtually the entire nation has subscribed to Irredentist aims and ideals—dream of an Italy whose northern frontier shall be formed by the main chain of the Alps, and whose rule shall be extended over the entire eastern shore of the Adriatic.

In order to intelligently understand the Italian view-point, suppose that we imagine ourselves in an analogous position. For this purpose you must picture Canada as a highly organized military Power, its policies directed by an aggressive, predacious and unscrupulous government, and with a population larger than that of the United States. You will conceive of the State of Vermont as a Canadian province under military control: a wedge driven into the heart of manufacturing New England, and threatening the teeming valleys of the Connecticut and the Hudson. You must imagine this province of Vermont as overrun by Canadian soldiery; as crisscrossed by military roads and strategic railways; its hills and mountains abristle with forts whose guns are turned United Statesward. The inhabitants of the province, though American in descent, in traditions, and in ideals, are oppressed by a harsh and tyrannical military rule. With the exception of a single trunk-line, there are no railways crossing the frontier. Commercial intercourse with the United States is virtually forbidden. To teach American history in the schools of Vermont is prohibited; to display the

American flag is a felony; to sing the "Star-Spangled Banner" is punishable by imprisonment or a fine. For the Vermonters to communicate, no matter how innocently, with their kinsmen in the United States, is to bring down upon them suspicion and possible punishment. By substituting Austria-Hungary for Canada, Italy for the United States, and the Trentino for Vermont, you will, perhaps, have a little clearer understanding of why the liberation of the Trentino from Austrian oppression is demanded by all Italians.

A similar homely parallel will serve to explain the Adriatic situation. You will imagine Seattle and the shores of Puget Sound, with its maze of islands, in Canadian possession. Seattle, Vancouver, and Victoria are strongly fortified bases for Canadian battle-fleets and flotillas of destroyers which constantly menace the commercial cities along our Pacific seaboard. The Americans dwelling in Seattle and the towns of the Olympic Peninsula are under an even harsher rule than their brethren in

Vermont. No American may hold a Government position. The Canadian authorities encourage and assist the immigration of thousands of Orientals in order to get the trade of the region out of American hands. A Canadian naval base at Honolulu threatens our trade routes in the Pacific and our commercial interests in Mexico and the Orient. In this analogy Seattle stands, of course, for Trieste; the Olympic Peninsula corresponds to the Istrian Peninsula; for Vancouver and Victoria you will read Pola and Fiume; while Honolulu might, by a slight exercise of the imagination, be translated into the great Austrian stronghold of Cattaro. Such is a reasonably accurate parallel to Italy's Adriatic problem.

For purposes of administration the Trentino, which the Austrians call Süd-Tirol, forms one province with Tyrol. For such a union there is no geographic, ethnologic, historic, or economic excuse. Of the 347,000 inhabitants of the Trentino, 338,000 are Italian. The half million inhabitants of Tyrol are, on the other hand, all Germans. The two regions are separated by a tremendous mountain wall, whose only gateway is the Brenner. On one side of that wall is Italy, with her vines, her mulberry-trees, her whitewashed, red-tiled cottages, her light-hearted, easy-going, Latin-blooded peasantry; across the mountains is the solemn, austere German scenery, with savage peaks and gloomy pine forests, a region inhabited by a stolid, slow-thinking Teutonic people. The Trentino and the Tyrol have about as much in common as Cuba and Maine.

The possession of the Trentino by Austria is not alone a geographical and ethnological anomaly: it is a pistol held at the head of Italy. Glance once more at the map, if you please, and you will see what I mean. The Trentino is, you will note, nothing but a prolongation of the valleys of Lombardy and Venetia. Held by Austria, it is like a great intrenched camp in the heart of northern Italy, menacing the valley of the Po, which is one of the kingdom's most vital arteries, and the link between her richest and most productive cities. From the Trentino, with its ring of forts, Austria can always threaten and invade her neighbor. She lies in the mountains, with the plains beneath her. She can always sweep down into the plains, but the Italians cannot seriously invade the mountains, since, even were they able to force the strongly defended passes, they would only find a maze of other mountains beyond. When, in the summer of 1916, the Archduke Frederick launched his great offensive from the Trentino, supported by a shattering artillery, he came perilously near—much nearer, indeed, than the world was permitted to know—to cutting the main east-and-west line of communications, which would have resulted in isolating the Italian armies operating on the Isonzo.

The Trentino is dominated by the army. Its administration is as essentially military in character as that of Gibraltar. It is, to all intents and purposes, one vast camp, commanded by thirty-five forts, gridironed with inaccessible military highways, and overrun with soldiery.

Economic expansion has been systematically discouraged. The waterfalls of the Trentino could, it is estimated, develop 250,000 horse-power, but the province has not benefited by this energy, for the regions to the north are already supplied, and the military authorities have not permitted its transmission to the manufacturing towns of Lombardy and Venetia, where it is needed. Neither roads nor railways have been built save for strategic purposes, and, as a result, the peasants have virtually no outlets for their produce. In fact, it has been the consistent policy of the Austrian Government to completely isolate the Trentino from Italy. In pursuance of this policy, all telephone and telegraph communications and many sorely needed railway connections with the other side of the frontier have been prohibited. Though the renting of their mountain pastures had always been the peasants' chief source of income, the military authorities issued orders, long before this war began, that Italian herdsmen could no longer drive their cattle across the border to graze, the prohibition being based on the ground that the herdsmen were really Italian army officers in disguise. In recent years the fear of Italian spies has become with the Austrian military authorities almost an insane obsession. Innocent tourists, engineers, and commercial travellers were arrested by the score on the charge of espionage. The mere fact of being an Italian was in itself ground for suspicion. Compared with the attitude of the Austrian Government toward its Italian subjects in the Trentino, the treatment accorded by the Boers to the British residents of the Transvaal was considerate and kind. Thus there arose in the Trentino, as in all Austrian provinces inhabited by Italians, a strange, unhealthy atmosphere of suspicion, of secrecy, and of fear. This atmosphere became so pronounced in recent years that it was sensed even by passing tourists, who felt as though they were in a besieged city, surrounded by secret agents and spies.

But, oppressive and tyrannical as are Austria's methods in the Trentino, the final expression of her anti-Italian policy is to be found in the Adriatic provinces. Here lie Austria's chief interests—the sea and commerce. Here, therefore, is to be found an even deeper fear of Italianism, and here still sterner methods are employed to stamp it out. The government of Trieste is, in fact, organized for that very purpose—witness the persecutions to which the citizens of Italian descent are subjected by the police, the countless political imprisonments, the systematic hostility to Italian schools in contrast to the Government's generosity toward German and Slovene institutions, and the State assistance given to Czech, Croatian, and Slovene banks for the purpose of taking the trade of the city out of Italian hands. Italians are excluded from all municipal employments, from the postal service, the railways, and the State industries. Nor does the official persecution end there. The presentation of many of the old Italian operas is forbidden. The singing of Garibaldi's Hymn leads to jail.

Every year thousands of Italian papers are confiscated. Until the war began hundreds of Italians were expelled annually by the police, to be replaced (according to the official instructions of 1912) "by more loyal and more useful elements."

Though for more than five centuries Trieste has belonged to the House of Hapsburg, the city is as Italian as though it had always been ruled from Rome. There is nothing in Trieste, save only the uniforms of the military and the *K.K.* on the doors of the Government offices, to remind one of Austrian rule. The language, the customs, the architecture, the names over the shop-doors, the faces of the people—everything is characteristically Italian. Outside of Trieste the zones of nationality are clearly divided: to the west, on the coast, dwell the Italians; in the mountainous interior to the eastward are the Slavs. But in Istria, that arrowhead-shaped peninsula at the head of the Adriatic, the population is almost solidly Italian. Though alternately bribed and bullied, cajoled and coerced, there persists, both among the simple peasants of the Trentino and Istria and the hard-headed business men of Trieste, a most sentimental and inextinguishable attachment for the Italian motherland. There is, indeed, something approaching the sublime in the fascination which Italy exercises across the centuries on these exiled sons of hers.

The arguments adduced by Italy for the acquisition of Dalmatia are by no means as sound ethnographically as her claims to the Trentino and Trieste. Though the apostles of expansion assert that ten per cent of the population of Dalmatia is Italian, this is an exaggeration, the most reliable authorities agreeing that the Italian element does not exceed three or four per cent. But this is not saying that Dalmatia is not, in spirit, in language, in traditions, Italian. Cruise along its shores, talk to its people, view the architecture of Ragusa, of Zara, of Spalato, and you will not need to be reminded that Dalmatia was Venetian until, little more than a century ago, Napoleon handed it over to Austria at the peace of Campo Formio in return for the recognition of his two made-to-order states, the Cis-Alpine and Ligurian Republics.

It is safe to say that the war will produce no more delicate problem than that of Dalmatia, which, as I have already shown, can never be settled on purely racial lines. Those who have studied the subject agree that to completely shut off Austria-Hungary from the sea would be a proceeding of grave unwisdom and one which would be certain to sow the seed for future wars. This is, I believe, the view taken by most deep-thinking Italians. The Italianization of the Adriatic's eastern seaboard would result, moreover, in raising a barrier against the legitimate expansion of the Balkan Slavs and would end the Serbian dream of an outlet to the sea. But the statesmen who are shaping Italy's policies are, I am convinced, too sensible and too far-seeing to commit so grave a blunder. Were I to hazard a prophecy—and prophesying is always a poor business—I should say that, no matter how conclusive a victory the Allies may achieve, neither Austria-Hungary nor Serbia will be wholly cut off from the salt water.

Events in the less remote theatres of war have prevented the Italian occupation of Albania from attracting the attention it deserves. The operations in that region have, moreover, been shrouded in mystery; foreigners desiring to visit Albania have met with polite but firm refusals; the published reports of the progress of the Albanian expedition—which, by the way, is a much larger force than is generally supposed—have been meagre and unsatisfying. The Italians figure, I fancy, on making their occupation as extensive and as solid as possible before the Albanian question comes up for international discussion.

If Italy's ambitions in Dalmatia bring her into collision with the Slavs, her plans for expansion in Albania are bound to arouse the hostility of the Greeks. The Italian troops at Argyocastro are occupying territory which Greece looks on as distinctly within her sphere of influence, and they menace Janina itself. Though Italy has intimated, I believe, that her occupation of Albania is not to be regarded as permanent, she is most certainly on the eastern shore of the Adriatic to stay, for her commercial and political interests will not permit her to have a Haiti or a Mexico at her front door. So I rather fancy that, when the peacemakers deal out the cards upon the green-topped table, Albania will become Italian in name, if not in fact, under a control similar to that which the French exercise in Morocco or the British in Egypt. And it will be quite natural, for there is in the Albanians a strong streak of Italian.

The settlement of this trans-Adriatic problem is going to require the most cautious and delicate handling. How far will Italy be permitted to go? How far may Serbia come? Shall Austria be cut off from the sea? Is Hungary to become an independent kingdom? Is Montenegro to disappear? What is Greece to get? The only one of these questions that can be answered with any certainty is the last.

Greece, as the result of her shifty and even treacherous attitude, will get very little consideration. On the decision of these questions hangs the future of the Balkan peoples. Though their final settlement must, of course, be deferred until the coming of peace, some regard will have to be paid, after all, to actual occupancies and accomplished facts. That is why Italy is making her position in Albania so solid that she cannot readily be ousted. And perhaps it is well that she is. Europe will owe a debt of gratitude to the Italians if they can bring law and order to Albania, which has never had a speaking acquaintance with either of them.

Nor do Italian ambitions end with the domination of the eastern shore of the Adriatic. With the destruction, or at least the disablement, of the Austrian Empire, Italy dreams of bringing within her political and commercial sphere of influence a considerable portion of the Balkan Peninsula, from which she is separated by only forty-seven miles of salt water.

But that is only the beginning of her vision of commercial greatness. Look at the map and you will see that with its continuation, the island of Sicily, Italy forms a great wharf which reaches out into the Mediterranean, nearly to the shores of Africa. Her peculiarly fortunate geographical position enables her, therefore, to offer the shortest route from Western and Central Europe to North Africa, the Levant, and the Farther East. It has been rumored, though with what truth I cannot say, that the Allies have agreed, in the event that they are completely victorious, to a rectification of the Tunisian and Egyptian frontiers, thus materially improving Italy's position in Libya, as the colony of Tripolitania is now known. It is also generally understood that, should the dismemberment of Asiatic Turkey be decided upon, the city of Smyrna, with its splendid harbor and profitable commerce, as well as a slice of the hinterland, will fall to Italy's portion. With her flag thus firmly planted on the coasts of three continents, with her most dangerous rival finally disposed of, with the splendid industrial organization, born of the war, speeded up to its highest efficiency, and with vast new markets in Africa, in Asia, in the Balkans opened to her products, Italy dreams of wresting from France and England the overlordship of the Middle Sea.

It would be useless to deny that an unfavorable impression was created in the United States by the fact that Italy, in entering the war, turned against her former allies. Her enemies have charged that she dickered with both the Entente and the Central Powers, and only joined the former because they made her the most tempting offer. That she did dicker with Austria is but the unvarnished truth—and of that chapter of Italian history the less said the better—but I am convinced that she finally entered the war, not because she had been bribed by promises of territorial concessions, but because the national conscience demanded that she join the forces of civilization in their struggle against barbarism. Suppose that I sketch for you, in brief, bold outline, the chain of historic events which occurred during the ten months between the presentation to Serbia of the Austrian ultimatum and Italy's declaration of war on Austria. Then you will be able to form your own opinion.

On the evening of July 23, 1914, Austria handed her note to Serbia. It demanded in overbearing and insulting terms that Serbia should place under Austrian control her schools, her law-courts, her police, in fact her whole internal administration. The little kingdom was given forty-eight hours in which to consider her answer. In other words, she was called upon, within the space of two days, to sacrifice her national independence. At six o'clock on the evening of July 25 the time limit allowed by the Austrian ultimatum expired. Half an hour later the Austrian Minister and his staff left Belgrade.

Now Article VII of the Treaty of Alliance between Italy, Austria, and Germany provided that in the event of any change in the *status quo* of the Balkan Peninsula which would entail a temporary or permanent occupation, Austria and Italy bound themselves to work in mutual accord on the basis of reciprocal compensation for any advantage, territorial or otherwise, obtained by either of the contracting Powers. Here is the text of the Article. Read it for yourself:

Austria-Hungary and Italy, who aim exclusively at the maintenance of the *status quo* in the East, bind themselves to employ their influence to prevent every territorial change which may be detrimental to one or other of the contracting Powers. They will give each other all explanations necessary for the elucidation of their respective intentions as well as those of the other Powers. If, however, in the course of events the maintenance of the *status quo* in the Balkans and on the Ottoman coasts and in the islands of the Adriatic and the Ægean Seas should become impossible, and if, either in consequence of the acts of a third Power or of other causes, Austria and Italy should be compelled to change the *status quo* by a temporary or permanent occupation, such occupation shall only take place after previous agreement between the two Powers, based on the principle of a reciprocal arrangement for all the advantages, territorial or other, which one of them may secure outside the *status quo,* and in such a manner as to satisfy all the legitimate claims of both parties.

Nothing could be plainer than that Austria-Hungary, by forcing war upon Serbia, planned to change the *status quo* in the Near East. Yet she had not taken the trouble to give Italy any explanation of her intentions, nor had she said anything about giving her ally reciprocal compensation as provided for in the treaty. Three days after the memorable 23d of July, therefore, Italy intimated to the Vienna Government that her idea of adequate compensation would be the cession of those Austrian provinces inhabited by Italians. In other words, she insisted that, if Austria was to extend her borders below the Danube by an occupation of Serbia, as was obviously her intention, thus upsetting the balance of power in the Balkans, Italy expected to receive as compensation the Trentino and Trieste, which, though under Austrian rule, are Italian in sentiment and population. Otherwise, she added, the Triple Alliance would be broken. On the 3d of August, having received no satisfactory reply from Austria, Italy declared her neutrality.

In so doing, however, she made it quite clear that she in no way admitted Austria's right to a free hand in the Adriatic or the Balkan Peninsula—regions which Italy has long regarded as within her own sphere of influence.

Early in the winter of 1914 Prince von Bülow, one of the most suave and experienced German diplomats, arrived in Rome on a special mission from Berlin. In his first interview with the Italian Minister of Foreign Affairs, Baron Sonnino, he frankly acknowledged Italy's right to territorial compensation under the terms of Article VII of the Triple Alliance. There is no doubt that Germany, recognizing the danger of flouting Italy, brought strong pressure to bear on Austria to surrender at least a portion of the regions in question. Austria, however, bluntly refused to heed either Italy's demands or Germany's suggestions. She refused even to discuss the question of ceding any part of her Italian provinces. She attempted, indeed, to reverse the situation by claiming compensation from Italy for the occu-

pation of the Dodecannesus and Vallona. The Dodecannesus was held as a pledge of Turkish good faith, while the occupation of Vallona was indispensable for the protection of Italian interests in Albania, where anarchy reigned, and where much the same conditions prevailed which existed in Mexico at the time of the American occupation of Vera Cruz.

The discussions might well have dragged on indefinitely, but late in March, 1915, Austria, goaded by her ally into a more conciliatory attitude, reluctantly consented to make concrete proposals. She offered to Italy the southern half of the Trentino, but mentioned no definite boundaries, and added that the bargain could not be carried into effect until peace had been concluded. In return she claimed from Italy heavy financial contributions to the National Debt and to the provincial and communal loans, also full indemnity for all investments made in the ceded territory, for all ecclesiastical property and entailed estates, and for the pensions of State officials. To assign even an ap-

proximate value to such concessions would entail a prolonged delay—a fact of which Austria was perfectly aware.

Italy responded to the Austrian advances by presenting her counter-claims, and for more than a month the negotiations pursued a difficult and tedious course. It must be admitted that, everything considered, Italy's claims were not particularly exorbitant. She claimed (1) a more extended and more easily defendable frontier in the Trentino, but she refrained from demanding the cession of the entire region lying south of the Brenner, as she would have been justified in doing from a strategic point of view; (2) a new boundary on the Isonzo which would give her possession of the towns of Gradisca and Gorizia (she has since taken them by arms); (3) the cession of certain islands of the Curzolari group; (4) the withdrawal of Austrian pretensions in Albania and the acknowledgement of Italy's right to occupy the Dodecannesus and Vallona; (5) the formation of the city of Trieste, together with the adjacent judicial districts of Priano and Capo d'Istria, into an autonomous State, independent of both Italy and Austria. By such an arrangement Austria would have retained nearly the whole of the Istrian Peninsula, the cities of Pola and Fiume, the entire Dalmatian coast, and the majority of the Dalmatian Islands. But she refused to even consider Italy's proposed changes in the Adriatic, or to do more than slightly increase her offer in the Trentino. Italy therefore broke off negotiations, and on May 4, 1915, the alliance with Austria was denounced.

Prince von Bülow was now confronted with the complete failure of his mission of keeping Italy yoked to Austria and Germany. No one realized better than this suave and astute diplomatist that the bonds which still held together the three nations were about to break. He next endeavored, by methods verging on the unscrupulous, to create distrust of the Italian Government among the Italian people. A member of the Reichstag circulated stealthily among the deputies and journalists, flattering each in turn with the assumption that he alone was the man of the moment, and offering him, in the names of Germany and Austria, new concessions which had not been communicated to the Italian Cabinet. It was back-stairs diplomacy in its shadiest and most questionable form. The concessions thus unofficially promised consisted of the offer of a new frontier in the Trentino, and for Trieste an administrative but not a political autonomy. The Adriatic, it seems, was to remain as before. And these concessions were all hedged about by impossible restrictions, or were not to come into effect until after the war. Yet at one time these intrigues came perilously near to accomplishing their purpose. Matters were still further complicated by the activities and interference of a former Foreign Minister, Signor Giolitti, whose vanity had been flattered, and whose ambitions had been cleverly played upon by the Teutonic emissary. To fully understand the extraordinary nature of this proceeding, one must picture Count von Bernstorff, at the height of the submarine crisis, negotiating not with the Government of the United States, but with Mr. William Jennings Bryan!

But, fortunately for the national honor, the Italian people, having had time to reflect what the future of Italy would be after the war, whatever its outcome, were they to be cut off from the only peoples in Europe with which they had spiritual sympathy, took things into their own hands. The storm of anger and indignation which swept the country rocked the Government to its foundations. The Salandra cabinet, which had resigned as a protest against the machinations of Giolitti, was returned to power. Through every city, town, and hamlet from Savoy to Sicily, thronged workmen, students, business and professional men, even priests and monks, waving the red-white-and-green banner and shouting the national watchwords "Italia Irredenta," and "Avanti Savoia!"

But there was a deeper cause underlying

these great patriotic demonstrations than mere hatred of Austria. They were expressions of national resentment at the impotent and dependent rôle which Italy had played so long. D'Annunzio, in one of his famous addresses in May, 1915, put this feeling into words: "We will no longer be a museum of antiquities, a kind of hostelry, a pleasure resort, under a sky painted over with Prussian blue, for the benefit of international honeymooners."

The sentiment of the people was expressed by the *Idea Nazionale,* which on May 10 declared:

> Italy desires war: (1) In order to obtain Trent, Trieste, and Dalmatia. The country desires it. A nation which has the opportunity to free its land should do so as a matter of imperative necessity. . . . (2) . . . in order to conquer for ourselves a good strategic frontier in the North and East. . . . (3) . . . because to-day, in the Adriatic, in the Balkan Peninsula, the Mediterranean, and Asia, Italy should have all the advantages it is possible for her to have, and without which her political, economic, and moral power would diminish in proportion as that of others increased. . . . If we would be a great Power we must accept certain obligations: one of them is war. . . .

The voice of the people was unmistakable: they wanted war. To have refused that demand would have meant the fall of the Government if not of the dynasty. The King did not want war. The responsible politicians, with a very few exceptions, did not want it. The nobility did not want it. The Church did not want it. The bankers and business men of the nation did not want it. It was the great mass of the Italian people, shamed and indignant at the position in which the nation had been placed by the sordid dickering with Austria, who swept the country into war. I was in Italy during those exciting days; I witnessed the impressive popular demonstrations in the larger cities; and in my mind there was left no shadow of a doubt that the Government had to choose between war and revolution. On the 23d of May, 1915, Italy declared war on Austria.

For ten months Italy, in the face of sneers and jeers, threats and reproaches, had maintained her neutrality. Be it remembered, however, that it was from the first a neutrality benevolent to the Allies. Even those who consider themselves well informed have apparently failed to recognize how decisive a factor that neutrality was. Italy's action in promptly withdrawing her forces from the French border relieved France's fears of an Italian invasion, and left her free to use the half million troops which had been guarding her southern frontier to oppose the German advance on Paris. It is not overstating the facts to assert that, had Italy's attitude toward France been less frank and honest, had the Republic not felt safe in stripping its southern border of troops, von Kluck would have broken through to Paris—he came perilously near to doing so as it was—and the whole course of the war would have been changed. It is to be hoped that, when the diplomatic history of the war comes to be written, the attitude of Italy during those critical days will receive the recognition which it deserves.

III

FIGHTING ON THE ROOF OF EUROPE

THE sun had scarcely shown itself above the snowy rampart of the Julian Alps when the hoarse throbbing of the big gray staff-car awoke the echoes of the narrow street on which fronts the Hotel Croce di Malta in Udine. Despite a leather coat, a fur-lined cap, and a great fleecy muffler which swathed me to the eyes, I shivered in the damp chill of the winter dawn. We adjusted our goggles and settled down into the heavy rugs, the soldier-driver threw in his clutch, the sergeant sitting beside him let out a vicious snarl from the horn, the little group of curious onlookers scattered hastily, and the powerful car leaped forward like a race-horse that feels the spur. With the horn sounding its hoarse warning, we thundered through the narrow, tortuous, cobble-paved streets, between rows of old, old houses

Alpini Going Into Action.

Their white uniforms make them almost indistinguishable against the blinding expanses of snow.

On the Roof of the World.

It not infrequently happens that the outposts on the higher peaks are cut off by a heavv fall of snow and cannot be relieved until the spring.

with faded frescoes on their plastered walls and with dim, echoing arcades. And so into the Piazza Vittorio Emanuele—there is no more charming little square in Italy—with its fountain and its two stone giants and the pompous statue of an incredibly ugly King astride a prancing horse and a monument to Peace set up by Napoleon to commemorate a treaty which was the cause of many wars. At the back of the piazza, like the back-drop on a stage, rises a towering sugar-loaf mound, thrown up, so they say, by Attila, that from it he might conveniently watch the siege and burning of Aquileia. Perched atop this mound, and looking for all the world like one of Maxfield Parrish's painted castles, is the Castello, once the residence of the Venetian and Austrian governors, and, rising above it, a white and slender tower. If you will take the trouble to climb to the summit of this tower you will find that the earth you left behind is now laid out at your feet like one of those putty maps you used to make in school. Below you, like a vast tessellated floor, is the Friulian plain, dotted with red-roofed villages, checkerboarded with fields of green and brown, stretching away, away to where, beyond the blue Isonzo, the Julian and Carnic Alps leap skyward in a mighty, curving, mile-high wall. You have the war before you, for amid those distant mountains snakes the Austro-Italian battle-line. Just as Attila and his Hunnish warriors looked down from the summit of this very mound, fourteen hundred years ago, upon the destruction of the Italian plain-towns, so to-day, from the same vantage-point, the Italians can see their artillery methodically pounding to pieces the defenses of the modern Huns. A strange reversal of history, is it not?

Leaving on our right the Palazzo Civico, built two-score years before Columbus set foot on the beach of San Salvador, we rolled through the gateway in the ancient city wall, acknowledging the salute of the steel-helmeted sentry just as the mail-clad knights who rode through that same gateway to the fighting on the plain, long centuries ago, doubtless acknowledged the salute of the steel-capped men-at-arms. Down the straight white road we sped, between rows of cropped and stunted willows, which line the highway on either side like soldiers with bowed heads. It is a storied and romantic region, this Venetia, whose fertile farm-lands, crisscrossed with watercourses, stretch away, flat and brown as an oaken floor, to the snowy crescent of the Alps. Scenes of past wars it still bears upon its face, in its farm-houses clustered together for common protection, in the stout walls and loopholed watch-towers of its towns, record of its warlike and eventful past. One must be prosaic indeed whose imagination remains unstirred by a journey across this historic plain, which has been invaded by Celts, Istrians, and Romans; Huns, Goths, and Lombards; Franks, Germans, and Austrians in turn. Over there, a dozen miles to the southward, lie the ruins of Aquileia, once one of the great cities of the western world, the chief outpost fortress of the Roman Empire, visited by King Herod of Judea, and the favorite residence of Augustus and Diocletian. These fertile lowlands were devastated by Alaric and his Visigoths and by Attila and his Huns—the original Huns, I mean. Down this very highroad tramped the legions of Tiberius on their way to give battle to the Illyrians and Pannonians. Here were waged the savage conflicts of the Guelphs, the Ghibellines, and the Scaligers. Here fought the great adventurer, Bartolommeo Colleoni; in the whitewashed village inn of Campo Formio, a far greater adventurer signed a treaty whereby he gave away the whole of this region as he would have given away a gold-piece; half a century later Garibaldi and his ragged redshirts fought to win it back.

For mile after mile we sped through a countryside which bore no suggestion of the bloody business which had brought me. So far as war was concerned, I might as well have been motoring through New England. But, though an atmosphere of tranquillity and security prevailed down here amid the villages and farmsteads of the plain, I knew that up there among those snow-crowned peaks ahead of us, musketry was crackling, cannon were belching, men were dying. But as we approached the front—though still miles and miles behind the fighting-line—the signs of war became increasingly apparent: base camps, remount depots, automobile parks, aviation schools, aerodromes, hospitals, machine-shops, ammunition-dumps, railway sidings chock-a-block with freight-cars and railway platforms piled high with supplies of every description. Moving closer, we came upon endless lines of motor-trucks moving ammunition and supplies to the front and other lines of motor-trucks and ambulances moving injured machinery and injured men to the repair-depots and hospitals at the rear. We passed Sicilian mule-carts, hundreds upon hundreds of them, two-wheeled, painted bright yellow or bright red and covered with gay little paintings such as one sees on ice cream venders' carts and hurdy-gurdies, the harness of the mules studded with brass and hung with scarlet tassels. Then long strings of donkeys, so heavily laden with wine-skins, with bales of hay, with ammunition-boxes, that all that could be seen of the animals themselves were their swinging tails and wagging ears. We met convoys of Austrian prisoners, guarded by cavalry or territorials, on their way to the rear. They looked tired and dirty and depressed, but most prisoners look that. A man who has spent days or even weeks amid the mud and blood of a trench, with no opportunity to bathe or even to wash his hands and face, with none too much food, with many of his comrades dead or wounded, with a shell-storm shrieking and howling about him, and has then had to surrender, could hardly be expected to appear high-spirited and optimistic. Yet it has long been the custom of the Allied correspondents and observers to base their assertions that the morale of the enemy is weakening and that the quality of his troops is deteriorating on the demeanor of prisoners fresh from the firing-line.

Ambulances passed us, travelling toward the hospitals at the base, and sometimes wounded men, limping along on foot. The heads of some were swathed in blood-stained bandages, some carried their arms in slings, others hobbled by with the aid of sticks, for the Italian army is none too well supplied with ambulances and those who are able to walk must do so in order that the places in the ambulances may be taken by their more seriously wounded fellows. They were dog-tired, dirty, caked with mud and blood, but they grinned at us cheerfully—for were they not beating the Austrians? Indeed, one cannot look at Italian troops without seeing that the spirit of the men is high and that they are confident of victory.

Now the roads became crowded, but never blocked, with troops on the march: infantry of the line, short, sturdily built fellows wearing short capes of greenish gray and trench-helmets of painted steel; Alpini, hardy and active as the goats of their own mountains, their tight-fitting breeches and their green felt hats with the slanting eagle's feather making them look like the chorus of *Robin Hood;* Bersaglieri, the flower of the Italian army, who have preserved the traditions of their famous corps by still clinging to the flat-brimmed, rakish hat with its huge bunch of drooping feathers; engineers, laden like donkeys with intrenching, bridging, and mining tools; motor-cycle despatch riders, leather-jacketed and mud-bespattered, the light-horsemen of modern war; and, very occasionally, for their hour for action has not yet come, detachments of cavalry, usually armed with lances, their helmets and busbies linen-covered to match the businesslike simplicity of their uniform. About the Italian army there is not much of the pomp and circumstance of war. It is as businesslike as a blued-steel revolver. In its total absence of swagger and display it is characteristic of a nation whose instincts are essentially democratic. Everything considered, the Italian troops compare very favorably with any in Europe. The men are for the most part shortish, very thick-set, and burned by the sun to the color of a much-used saddle. I rather expected to see bearded, unkempt fellows, but I found them clean-shaven and extraordinarily neat. The Italian military authorities do not approve of the *poilu.* Though the men are laden like pack-mules, they cover the ground at a surprisingly smart pace, while special corps, such as the Bersaglieri and the Alpini, are famous for the fashion in which they take even the steepest acclivities at the double. I was told that, though the troops recruited in the North possess the most stamina and endurance, the Neapolitans and Sicilians have the most *élan* and make the best fighters, these sons of the South having again and again advanced to the assault through storms of fire which the colder-blooded Piedmontese refused to face.

It is claimed for the Italian uniform that it is at once the ugliest and the least visible of any worn in Europe. "Its wearer doesn't even make a shadow," a friend of mine remarked. The Italian military authorities were among the first to make a scientific study of colors for uniforms. They did not select, for example, the "horizon blue" adopted by the French because, while this is less visible on the roads and plains of a flat, open, sunlit region, it would prove fatally distinct on the tree-clad mountain slopes where the Italians are fighting. The color is officially described as gray-green, but the best description of it is that given by a British officer: "Take some mud from the Blue Nile, carefully rub into it two pounds of ship-rat's hair, paint a roan horse with the composition, and then you will understand why the Austrians can't see the Italian soldiers in broad daylight at fifty yards." Its quality of invisibility is, indeed, positively uncanny. While motoring in the war zone I have repeatedly come upon bodies of troops resting beside the road, yet, so marvellously do their uniforms merge into the landscape that, had not my attention been called to them, I should have passed them by unnoticed. The uniform of the Italian officer is of precisely the same cut and apparently of the same material as that of the men, and as the former not infrequently dispenses with the badges of rank, it is often difficult to distinguish an officer from a private. The Italian officers, particularly those of the cavalry regiments, have always been among the smartest in Europe, but the gorgeous uniforms which, in the happy, carefree days before the war, added such brilliant notes of color to the scenes on the Corso and in the Cascine, have been replaced by a dress which is as simple as it is serviceable.

The Italian Government has a stern objection to wasteful or unnecessary expenditure, and all the costly and superfluous trimmings so dear to the heart of the military have been ruthlessly pruned. But economy is not insisted upon at the expense of efficiency. Nothing is refused or stinted that is necessary to keep the soldiers in good health or that will add to the efficiency of the great fighting-machine. But the war is proving a heavy financial strain for Italy and she is determined not to waste on it a single soldo more than she can possibly help. On the French and British fronts staff-officers are constantly dashing to and fro in motor-cars on errands of more or less importance. But you see nothing of that sort in the Italian war zone. The Comando Supremo can, of course, have all the motor-cars it wants, but it discourages their use except in cases of necessity. The officers are instructed that, whenever they can travel by railway without detriment to the interests of the service, they are expected to do so, for the trains are in operation to within a few miles of the front and with astonishing regularity, whereas tires and gasolene cost money. Returning at nightfall from the front to Udine, we were nearly always stopped by officers—majors, colonels, and once by a general—who would ask us to give them a lift into town. It has long been the fashion among foreigners to think of Italians, particularly those of the upper class, as late-rising, easy-going, and not particularly in love with work—a sort of *dolce far niente* people. But the war has shown how unsafe are such generalizations. There is no harder worker on any front than the Italian officer. Even the highest staff-officers are at their desks by eight and frequently by seven. Though it is easier to get from the Italian front to Milan or Florence than it is to get from Verdun to Paris, or from the Somme to London, one sees little of the week-end travelling so common on the British front. Officers in the war zone are entitled to fifteen days' leave of absence a year, and from this rule there are no deviations.

Through the mud we came to the Judrio, which marked the line of the old frontier. We crossed the river by a pontoon bridge, for the Austrians had destroyed the other in their retreat.

"We are in Austria now, I suppose?" I remarked. "In Italia Redenta," my companion corrected me. "This region has always been Italian in everything but name, and now it is Italian in name also." The occupation by the Italian troops, at the very outset of the war, of this wedge of territory between the Judrio and the Isonzo, with Monfalcone, Cervignano, Cormons, Gradisca—old Italian towns all—did much to give the Italian people confidence in the efficiency of their armies and the ability of their generals.

Now the roads were filled with the enormous equipment of an army advancing. Every village swarmed with gray soldiers. We passed interminable processions of motor-lorries, mule-carts, trucks, and wagons piled high with hay,* lumber, wine-casks, flour, shells, barbed wire; boxes of ammunition; pontoon-trains, balloon outfits, searchlights mounted on motor-trucks, wheeled blacksmith shops, wheeled post-offices, field-kitchens; beef and mutton on the hoof; mammoth howitzers and siege guns hauled by panting tractors; creaking, clanking field-batteries, and bright-eyed, brown-skinned, green-caped infantry, battalions, regiments,

* I was told by a British general that thousands of tiny steel prongs had been discovered in baled hay brought from America. They were evidently put there by German sympathizers in the United States with the object of killing the Allies' horses.

A Heavy Howitzer in the High Alps.

Nowadays guns "command" nothing. Instead of frowning down on the enemy from an eminence, they stare blindly skyward from behind a wall of mountains.

An Outpost in the Carnia.

"On no front, not on the sun-scorched plains of Mesopotamia, nor in the Masurian marshes, nor in the blood-soaked mud of Flanders, does the fighting man lead so arduous an existence as up here on the roof of the world."

brigades of them plodding along under slanting lines of steel. All the resources of Italy seemed crowding up to make good the recent gains and to make ready for the next push. One has to see a great army on the march to appreciate how stupendous is the task of supplying with food the hungry men and the hungrier guns, and how it taxes to the utmost all the industrial resources of a nation.

Under all this traffic the roads remained hard and smooth, for gangs of men, with scrapers and steam-rollers were at work everywhere repairing the wear and tear. This work is done by peasants, who are too old for the army, middle-aged, sturdily built fellows who perform their prosaic task with the resignation and inexhaustible patience of the lower-class Italian. They are organized in companies of a hundred men each, called *centurias,* and the company commanders are called (shades of the Roman legions!) *centurions.* Italy owes much to these gray-haired soldiers of the pick and shovel who, working in heat and cold, in snow and rain, and frequently under Austrian fire, have made it possible for the armies to advance and for food to be sent forward for the men and ammunition for the guns.

When this war is over Italy will find herself with better roads, and more of them, than she ever had before. The hundreds of miles of splendid highways which have been built by the army in the Trentino, in the Carnia, and in Cadore will open up districts of extraordinary beauty which have hitherto been inaccessible to the touring motorist. The Italians have been fortunate in having an inexhaustible supply of road-building material close at hand, for the mountains are solid road metal and in the plains one has only to scratch the soil to find gravel. The work of the road-builders on the Upper Isonzo resembles a vast suburban development, for the smooth white highways which zigzag in long, easy gradients up the mountain slopes are bordered on the inside by stone-paved gutters and on the outside, where the precipice falls sheer away, by cut stone guard-posts. So extensive and substantial are these improvements that one instinctively looks for a real-estate dealer's sign: "This beautiful lot can be yours for twenty-five dollars down and ten dollars a month for a year." Climbing higher, the roads become steeper and narrower and, because of the heavy rains, very highly crowned, with frequent right-angle and hair-pin turns. Here a skid or a side-slip or the failure of your brakes is quite likely to bring your career to an abrupt and unpleasant termination. To motor along one of these military mountain highways when it is slippery from rain is as nerve-trying as walking on a shingled roof with smooth-soled shoes. At one point on the Upper Isonzo there wasn't enough room between our outer wheels and the edge of the precipice for a starved cat to pass.

Now we were well within the danger zone. I knew it by the screens of woven reeds and grass matting which had been erected along one side of the road in order to protect the troops and transport using that road from being seen by the Austrian observers and shelled by the Austrian guns. Practically all of the roads on the Italian side of the front are, remember, under direct observation by the Austrians. In fact, they command everything. Everywhere they are above the Italians. From the observatories which they have established on every peak they can see through their powerful telescopes what is transpiring down on the plain as readily as though they were circling above it in an airplane. As a result of the extraordinary advantage which the Austrians enjoy in this respect, it has been found necessary to screen certain of the roads not only on both sides but above, so that in places the traffic passes for miles through literal tunnels of matting. This road masking is a simple form of the art of concealment to which the French have given the name *"camouflage,"* which has been developed to an extraordinary degree on the Western Front. That the Italians have not made a greater use of it is due, no doubt, to the wholly different conditions under which they are fighting.

Now the crowded road that we were following turned sharply into a narrow valley, down which a small river twisted and turned on its way to the sea. Though the Italian positions ran along the top of the hill slope just above us, and though less than a thousand yards away were the Austrian trenches, that valley, for many miles, was literally crawling with men and horses and guns. Indeed it was difficult to make myself believe that we were within easy range of the enemy and that at any instant a shell might fall upon that teeming hillside and burst with the crash that scatters death.

Despite the champagne-cork popping of the rifles and the basso profundo of the guns, it was a scene of ordered, yes, almost peaceful industry which in no way suggested war but reminded me, rather, of the Panama Canal at the busiest period of its construction (I have used the simile before, but I use it again because I know none better), of the digging of the New

York subway, of the laying of a transcontinental railway, of the building of the dam at Assuan. Trenches which had recently been captured from the Austrians were being cleared and renovated and new trenches were being dug, roads were being repaired, a battery of monster howitzers was being moved into ingeniously concealed positions, a whole system of narrow-gauge railway was being laid down, enormous quantities of stores were being unloaded from wagons and lorries and neatly stacked, soldiers were building great water-tanks on stilts, like those at railway sidings, giant shells were being lowered from trucks and flat-cars by means of cranes; to the accompaniment of saws and hammers a city of wooden huts was springing up on the reverse slope of the hill as though at the wave of a magician's wand.

As I watched with fascinated eyes this scene of activity, as city idlers watch the laborers at work in a cellar excavation, a shell burst on the crowded hillside, perhaps five hundred yards away. There was a crash like the explosion of a giant cannon-cracker; the ground leaped into flame and dust. A few minutes afterward I saw an ambulance go tearing up the road.

"Just a chance shot," said the staff-officer who accompanied me. "This valley is one of the few places on our front which is invisible to the Austrian observers. That's why we have so many troops in here. The Austrian aviators could spot what is going on here, of course, but our fliers and our anti-aircraft batteries have been making things so hot for them lately that they're not troubling us much. That's the great thing in this game—to keep control of the air. If the Austrian airmen were able to get over this valley and direct the fire of their guns we wouldn't be able to stay here an hour."

My companion had thought that it might be possible to follow the road down the valley to Monfalcone and the sea, and so it would have been had the weather continued misty and rainy. But the sun came out brightly just as we reached the beginning of an exposed stretch of the road; an Austrian observer, peering through a telescope set up in a monastery on top of a mountain ten miles away, caught sight of the hurrying gray insect which was our car; he rang up on the telephone a certain battery and spoke a few words to the battery commander; and an instant later on the road along which we were travelling Austrian shells began to fall. Shells being expensive, that little episode cost the Emperor-King several hundred kronen, we figured. As for us, it merely interrupted a most interesting morning's ride.

Leaving the car in the shelter of a hill, we toiled up a steep and stony slope to a point from which I was able to get an admirable idea of the general lay of Italy's Eastern Front. Coming toward me was the Isonzo—a bright blue stream the width of the Thames at New London—which, happy at escaping from its gloomy mountain defile, went rioting over the plain in a great westward curve. Turning, I could catch a glimpse, through a notch in the hills, of the white towers and pink roofs of Monfalcone against the Adriatic's changeless blue. To the east of Monfalcone rose the red heights of the Carso, the barren limestone plateau which stretches from the Isonzo south into Istria. And beyond the Carso I could trace the whole curve of the mountains from in front of Trieste up past Gorizia and away to the Carnia. The Italian front, I might add, divides itself into four sectors: the Isonzo, the Carnia and Cadore, the Trentino, and the Alpine.

Directly below us, not more than a kilometre away, was a village which the Austrians were shelling. Through our glasses we could see the effects of the bombardment as plainly as though we had been watching a football game from the upper tier of seats in the Yale Bowl. They were using a considerable number of guns of various calibers and the crash of the bursting shells was almost incessant. A shell struck a rather pretentious building, which was evidently the town hall; there was a burst of flame, and a torrent of bricks and beams and tiles shot skyward amid a geyser of green-brown smoke. Another projectile chose as its target the tall white campanile, which suddenly slumped into the street, a heap of brick and plaster. Now and again we caught glimpses of tiny figures—Italian soldiers, most likely—scuttling for shelter. Occasionally the Austrians would vary their rain of heavy projectiles with a sort of shell that went *bang* and released a fleecy cloud of smoke overhead and then dropped a parcel of high explosive that burst on the ground. It was curious to think that the guns from which these shells came were cunningly hidden away in nooks and glens on the other side of that distant range of hills, that the men serving the guns had little if any idea what they were firing at, and that the bombardment was being directed and controlled by an officer seated comfortably at the small end of a telescope up there on a mountain top among the clouds. Yet such is modern war. It used to be one of the artillerist's tenets that his guns should be placed in a position with a "commanding" range of view. But nowadays guns "command" nothing. Instead they are tucked away in gullies and leafy glens and excavated gun-pits, and their muzzles, instead of frowning down on the enemy from an eminence, stare blindly skyward from behind a wall of hills or mountains. The Italians evidently grew tired of letting the Austrians have their way with the town, for presently some batteries of heavy guns behind us came into action and their shells screamed over our heads. Soon a brisk exchange of compliments between the Italian and Austrian guns was going on over the shattered roofs of the town. We did not remain overlong on our hillside and we were warned by the artillery officer who was guiding us to keep close to the ground and well apart, for, were the Austrians to see us in a group, using maps and field-glasses, they probably would take us for artillery observers and would send over a violent protest cased in steel.

On none of the European battle-fronts is

there a more beautiful and impressive journey than that from Udine up to the Italian positions in the Carnia. The Carnia sector connects the Isonzo and Trentino fronts and forms a vital link in the Italian chain of defense, for, were the Austrians to break through, they would take in flank and rear the great Italian armies operating on the two adjacent fronts. West of the Carnia, in Cadore, the Italians are campaigning in one of the world's most famous playgrounds, for, in the days before the Great War, pleasure-seekers from every corner of Europe and America swarmed by the tens of thousands in the country round about Cortina and in the enchanted valleys of the Dolomites. But now great gray guns are emplaced in the shady glens where the honeymooners used to stroll; on the terraces of the tourist hostelries, where, on summer afternoons, men in white flannels and women in dainty frocks chattered over their tea, now lounge Italian officers in field uniforms of gray; the blare of dance music and the popping of champagne corks has been replaced by the blare of bugles and the popping of rifles.

If you have ever gone, in a single day, from the sunlit orange groves of Pasadena up to the snow-crowned peaks of the Coast Range, you will have as good an idea as I can give you of the journey from the Isonzo up to the Carnia. Down on the Carso the war is being waged under a sky of molten brass and in summer the winds which sweep that arid plateau are like blasts from an open furnace-door. The soldiers fighting in the Carnia, on the other hand, not infrequently wear coats of white fur to protect them from the cold and to render them invisible against the expanses of snow. When I was on the Italian front they told me an incident of this mountain warfare. There was desperate fighting for the possession of a few yards of mountain trenches and a half-battalion of Austrian Jaegers—nearly five hundred men—were enfiladed by machine-gun fire and wiped out. That night there was a heavy snowfall and the Austrian corpses sprawled upon the mountainside were soon buried deep beneath the fleecy flakes. The long winter wore along, the war pursued its dreary course, to five hundred Austrian homes the Austrian War Office sent a brief message that the husband or son or brother had been "reported missing." Then the spring came, the snow melted from the mountainsides, and the horrified Italians looked on the five hundred Austrians, frozen stiff, as meat is frozen in a refrigerator, in the same attitudes in which they had died months before.

With countless hair-pin, hair-raising turns, our road wound upward, bordered on one hand by the brinks of precipices, on the other by bare walls of rock. It was a smooth road, splendidly built, but steep and terrifyingly narrow—so narrow in places that it was nothing more than a shelf blasted from the sheer face of the cliff. Twice, meeting motor-lorries downward bound, we had to back along that narrow shelf, with our outer wheels on the brink of emptiness, until we came to a spot where there was room to pass. It was a ticklish business.

At one point a mountain torrent leaped from the cliff into the depths below. But the water-power was not permitted to go to waste; it had been skilfully harnessed and was being used to run a completely equipped machine-shop where were brought for repair everything from motor-trucks to machine-guns. That was one of the things that impressed me most—the mechanical ability of the Italians. The railways, cable-ways, machine-shops, bridges, roads, reservoirs, concrete works that they have built, more often than not in the face of what would appear to be unsurmountable difficulties, prove them to be a nation of engineers.

Up to the heights toward which we were climbing so comfortably and quickly in a motor-car there was before the war, so I was told, nothing but a mule-path. Now there is this fine military road, so ingeniously graded and zigzagged that two-ton motor-trucks can now go with ease where before a donkey had difficulty in finding a footing. When these small and handy motor-trucks come to a point where it is no longer possible for them to find traction, their loads are transferred to the remarkable wire-rope railways, or *teleifericas,* as they are called, which have made possible this campaign in cloudland. Similar systems are in use, all over the world, for conveying goods up the sides of mountains and across chasms. A wire rope running over a drum at each side of the chasm which has to be crossed forms a double line of overhead railway. Suspended on grooved wheels from this overhead wire are "cars" consisting of shallow iron trays about the length and width of coffins, one car going up as the other comes down. The floors of the cars are perforated so as to permit the draining off of water or blood—for men wounded in the mountain fighting are frequently brought down to the hospitals in them—and the sides are of latticework, and, I might add, quite unnecessarily low. Nor is the prospective passenger reassured by being told that there have been several cases where soldiers, suddenly overcome by vertigo, have thrown themselves out while in mid-air. If the cars are properly loaded, and if there is not a high wind blowing, the *tele-ferica* is about as safe as most other modes of conveyance, but should the cars have been care-lessly loaded, or should a strong wind be blow-ing, there is considerable danger of their com-ing into collision as they pass. In such an event there would be a very fair chance of the pas-senger spattering up the rocks a thousand feet or so below. There is still another, though a rather remote possibility: that of being shelled while in mid-air, for certain of the *telefericas* run within view of the Austrian positions. And sometimes the power which winds the drum gives out and the car and its passengers are temporarily marooned in space. Aviation, motor-racing, mountain-climbing, big-game hunting, all seem commonplace and tame compared with the sensation of swinging help-lessly in a shallow bathtub over half a mile of emptiness while an Austrian battery endeavors to pot you with shrapnel, very much as a small boy throws stones at a scared cat clinging to a limb.

Yet over these slender wires has been transported an army, with its vast quantities of food, stores, and ammunition, and by the same method of transportation have been sent back the wounded. Without this ingenious device it is doubtful if the campaign in the High Alps could ever have been fought. But the cables, strong though they are, are yet too weak to bear the weight of the heavy guns, some of them weighing forty and fifty tons, which the Italians have put into action on the highest peaks. So, by the aid of ropes and levers and pulleys and hundreds of brawny backs and straining arms, these monster pieces have been hauled up slopes as steep as that of the Great Pyramid, have been hoisted up walls of rock as sheer and high as those of the Flatiron Building. You question this? Well, there they are, great eight and nine inch monsters, high above the highest of the wire roads, one of them that I know of at a height of ten thousand feet above the sea. There is no doubting it, incredible as it may seem, for they speak for themselves—as the Austrians have found to their cost.

The most advanced positions in the Carnia, as in the Trentino, are amid the eternal snows. Here the guns are emplaced in ice caverns which can be reached only through tunnels cut through the drifts; here the men spend their days wrapped in shaggy furs, their faces smeared with grease as a protection from the stinging blasts, and their nights in holes burrowed in the snow, like the igloos of Esquimaux. On no front, not on the sun-scorched plains of Mesopotamia, nor in the frozen Mazurian marshes, nor in the blood-soaked mud of Flanders, does the fighting man lead so arduous an existence as up here on the roof of the world. I remember standing with an Italian officer in an observatory in the lower mountains. The powerful telescope was trained on the snow-covered summit of one of the higher peaks.

"Do you see that little black speck on the snow at the very top?" the officer asked me.

I told him that I did.

"That is one of our positions," he continued. "It is held by a lieutenant and thirty Alpini. I have just received word that, as the result of yesterday's snow-storm, our communications with them have been cut off. We will not be able to relieve them, or get supplies to them, much before next April."

And it was then only the middle of December!

In the Carnia and on the Upper Isonzo one finds the anomaly of first-line trenches which are perfectly safe from attack. I visited such a position. Through a loophole I got a little framed picture of the Austrian trenches not five hundred yards away, and above them, cut in the mountainside, the square black openings within which lurked the Austrian guns. Yet we were as safe from anything save artillery fire as though we were in Mars, for between the Italian trenches and the Austrian intervened a chasm half a thousand feet deep and with walls as steep and smooth as the side of a house. The narrow strip of valley at the bottom of the chasm was a sort of no man's land, where forays, skirmishes, and all manner of desperate adventures took place nightly between patrols of Jaegers and Alpini.

As with my field-glasses I was sweeping the turmoil of trench-scarred mountains which lay spread, below me, like a map in bas-relief, an Austrian battery quite suddenly set up a deafening clamor, and on a hillside, miles away, I could see its shells bursting in clouds of smoke shot through with flame. They looked like gigantic white peonies breaking suddenly into bloom. The racket of the guns awoke the most extraordinary echoes in the mountains. It was difficult to believe that it was not thunder. Range after range caught up the echoes of that bombardment and passed them on until it seemed as though they must have reached Vienna. For half an hour, perhaps, the cannonade continued, and then, from an Italian position somewhere above and behind us, came a mighty bellow which drowned out all other sounds. It was the angry voice of Italy bidding the Austrians be still.

CHAPTER IV

THE ROAD TO TRIESTE

IN order to appraise the Italian operations on the Carso at their true value, it is necessary to go back to May, 1916, when the Archduke Frederick launched his great offensive from the Trentino. Now it must be kept constantly in mind, as I have tried to emphasize in preceding chapters, that when the war opened, the Italians had always to go up while the Austrians needed only to come down. The latter, intrenched high on that tremendous natural rampart formed by the Rhaetian and Tyrolean Alps, the Dolomites, the Carnic, Julian, and Dinaric ranges, had an immense superiority over their enemy on the plains below. The Austrian offensive in the Trentino was dictated by four reasons: first, to divert the Italians from their main objective, Trieste; second, to lessen the pressure which General

Cadorna was exerting against the Austrian lines on the Isonzo; third, to smash through to Vicenza and Verona, thus cutting off and compelling the capitulation of the Italian armies operating in Venetia; and fourth, to so thoroughly discourage the Italians that they would consent to a separate peace.

The story of how this ambitious plan was foiled is soon told. By the first week in May the Austrians had massed upon the Trentino front a force of very nearly 400,000 men with 2,000 guns. Included in this tremendous accumulation of artillery were 26 batteries of 12-inch guns and several of the German giants, the famous 42-centimetre pieces, which brought down the pride of Antwerp and Namur. By the middle of May everything was ready for the onset to begin, and this avalanche of soldiery came rolling down the Asiago plateau, between the Adige and the Brenta. Below them, basking in the sunshine, stretched the alluring plains of Venetia, with their wealth, their women, and their wine. Pounded by an immensely superior artillery, over-whelmed by wave upon wave of infantry, the Italians sullenly fell back, leaving the greater part of the Sette Communi plateau and the upper portion of the Brenta valley in the hands of the Austrians. At the beginning of June a cloud of despondency and gloom hung over Italy, and men went about with sober faces, for it seemed all but certain that the enemy would succeed in breaking through to Vicenza, and by cutting the main east-and-west line of railway, would force the armies operating on the Isonzo and in the Carnia to surrender. But the soldiers of the Army of the Trentino, though outnumbered in men and guns, deter-mined that the Austrians should pay a stag-gering price for every yard of ground they gained. They fought as must have fought their ancestors of the Roman legions. And, thanks to their tenacity and pluck, they held their opponents on the five-yard line. Then, just in the nick of time, the whistle blew. The game was over. The Austrians had to hurry home.

They had staked everything on a sudden and overwhelming onslaught by which they hoped to smash the Italian defense and demoralize the Italian armies in time to permit at least half their eighteen divisions and nearly all of their heavy guns being withdrawn in a few weeks and rushed across Austria to the Galician front, where they were desperately needed to stay the Russian advance.

By the beginning of the last week in June the Austrian General Staff, recognizing that its plan for the overwhelming of northern Italy had failed disastrously, issued orders for a general retreat. The Austrians had planned to fall back on the positions which had been prepared in advance in the mountains and to establish themselves, with greatly reduced numbers, on this practically impregnable line, while the transfer of the divisions intended for the Carpathians was effected. But General Cadorna had no intention of letting the Austrians escape so easily. In less than a week he had collected from the garrisons and training camps and reserve battalions an army of 500,000 men. It was one of the most remarkable achievements of the war. From all parts of Italy he rushed those half million men to the Trentino front by train—and despite the immense strain put upon the Italian railways by the rapid movement of so great a body of troops, the regular passenger service was suspended for only three days. (At that same time the American Government was attempting to concentrate a force of only 150,000 men on the Mexican border; a comparison of Italian and American efficiency is instructive.) He formed that army into brigades and divisions, each complete with staff and supply trains and ammunition columns. He organized fresh bases of supply, including water, of which there is none on the Asiago plateau. He provided the stupendous quantity of stores and ammunition and equipment and transport required by such an army. (It is related how Cadorna's Chief of Transport wired the Fiat Company of Turin that he must have 545 additional motor-trucks within a week, and how that great company responded by delivering in the time specified 546—one over for good measure.) Almost in a night he transformed the rude mule-paths leading up onto the plateau into splendid military roads, wide enough and hard enough to bear the tremendous traffic to which they were suddenly subjected. And finally he rushed his troops up those roads in motor-cars and motor-trucks, afoot and on horse-back and astride of donkeys and flung them against the Austrians. So sudden and savage was the Italian onset that the Austrians did not dare to spare a man or gun for their Eastern Front—and meanwhile the Muscovite armies were pressing on toward the Dniester. It is no exaggeration to assert that the success of Brussiloff's offensive in Galicia was due in no small measure to the Italian counter-offensive in the Trentino. That adventure cost Austria at least 100,000 dead and wounded men.

But not for a moment did the Italians permit the Austrian offensive in the Trentino to distract them from their real objectives: Gorizia, the Carso, and Trieste. The "military experts," who from desks in newspaper offices tell the public how campaigns ought to be conducted, had announced confidently that Italy had so taxed her strength by her efforts in the Trentino that, for many months at least, nothing need be expected from her. But Italy showed the public that the "military experts" didn't know what they were talking about, for in little more than a month after the Italian guns had ceased to growl amid the Tyrolean peaks and passes, they were raining a storm of steel upon the Austrian positions on the Carso.

Imagine a vast limestone plateau, varying in height from 700 to 2,500 feet, which is as treeless and waterless as the deserts of Chihuahua, as desolate and forbidding as the Dakota Bad Lands, with a surface as torn and twisted and jagged as the lava beds of Utah, and with a summer climate like that of Death Valley in July. That is the Carso. This great tableland of rock, which begins at Gorizia, approaches close to the shores of the Adriatic between Monfalcone and Trieste, and runs southeastward into Istria, links the Alpine system with the Balkan ranges. Its surface of naked, sun-flayed rock is broken here and there with gigantic heaps of piled stone, with caves and caverns, with sombre marshes which sometimes become gloomy and forbidding lakes, and with peculiar crater-like depressions called *dolinas,* formed by centuries of erosion. Such scanty vegetation as there is is confined to these *dolinas,* which form the only oases in this barren and thirsty land. The whole region is swept by the *Bora,* a wind which is the enemy alike of plant and man. Save for the lizards that bask upon its furnace-like floors, the Carso is as lifeless as it is treeless and waterless. No bird and scarcely an insect can find nourishment over vast spaces of this sun-scorched solitude; even the hardy mountain grass withers and dies of a broken heart. So powerful is the sun that eggs can be cooked without a fire. Metal objects, such as rifles and equipment, when left exposed, quickly become too hot to touch. The bodies of the soldiers who fall on the Carso are not infrequently found to have been baked hard and mummified after lying for a day or two on that oven-like floor of stone.

The Carso is probably the strongest natural fortress in the world. Anything in the shape of defensive works which Nature had overlooked, the Austrians provided. For years before the war began the Austrian engineers were at work strengthening a place that already possessed superlative strength. The whole face of the plateau was honeycombed with trenches and tunnels and dugouts and gun emplacements which were blasted and drilled out of the solid rock with machinery similar to that used in driving the Simplon and the St. Gothard tunnels. The posts for the snipers were armored with inch-thick plates of steel cemented into the rock. The *dolinas* were converted into machine-gun pits and bomb-proof shelters. In one of these curious craters I saw a dugout—it was really a subterranean barracks—electrically lighted and with neatly whitewashed walls which had sleeping accommodation for a thousand men. To supply these positions, water was pumped up by oil-engines, but the Austrians took care to destroy the pipelines as they retired.

At the northern end of the Carso, in an angle formed by the junction of the Wippach and the Isonzo, the snowy towers and red-brown roofs of Gorizia rise above the foliage of its famous gardens. The town, which resembles Homburg or Baden-Baden and was a popular Austrian resort before the war, lies in the valley of the Wippach (Vippacco, the Italians call it), which separates the Carso from the southernmost spurs of the Julian Alps. Down this valley runs the railway leading to Trieste, Laibach, and Vienna. It will be seen, therefore, that Gorizia is really the gateway to Trieste, and a place of immense strategic importance.

On the slopes of the Carso, four or five miles to the southwest of the town, rises the enormously strong position of Monte San Michele, and a few miles farther down the Isonzo, the fortified hill-town of Sagrado. On the other side of the river, almost opposite Gorizia, are the equally strong positions of Podgora and Monte Sabotino. Their steep slopes were slashed with Austrian trenches and abristle with guns which commanded the roads leading to the river, the bridge-heads, and the town. To take Gorizia until these positions had been captured was obviously out of the question. Here, as elsewhere, Austria held the upper ground. In a memorandum issued by the Austrian General Staff to its officers at the beginning of the operations before Gorizia, the tremendous advantage of the Austrian position was made quite clear: "We have to retain possession of a terrain fortified by Nature. In front of us a great watercourse; behind us a ridge from which we can shoot as from a ten-story building."

The difficulties which the Italians had to overcome in their advance were enormous.

From their mountain nests the Austrian guns were able to maintain a murderous fire on the Italian lines of communication, thus preventing the bringing up of men and supplies. It therefore became necessary for the Italians to build new roads which would not be thus exposed to enemy fire, and in cases where this was impossible, the existing roads were masked for miles on end with artificial hedges and screens of grass matting. In many places it was found necessary to screen the roads overhead as well as on the sides, so that the Italians could move up their heavy guns without attracting the attention of the enemy's observers stationed on the highest mountain peaks, or of the Austrian airmen. But this was not all, or nearly all. An army is ever a hungry monster, so slaughter-houses and bakeries and field-kitchens, to say nothing of incredible quantities of food-stuffs, had to be provided. Fighting being a thirsty business, it was necessary to arrange for piping up water, for great tanks to hold that water, and for water-carts, hundreds and hundreds of

them, to peddle it among the panting troops. A prize-fighter cannot sleep out in the open, on the bare ground, and keep in condition for the ring, and a soldier, who is likewise a fighting-man but from a different motive, must be made comfortable of nights if he is to keep in fighting-trim. So millions of feet of lumber had to be brought up, along roads already overcrowded with traffic, and that lumber had to be transformed into temporary huts and barrackments—a city of them. But the preparations did not end even there. To insure the co-ordination and co-operation of the various divisions of the army, an elaborate system of field telegraphs and telephones had to be installed, and, in order to provide against the lines being cut by shell-fire and the whole complex organism paralyzed, the wires were laid in groups of four. Then there had to be repair-stations for the broken machinery, and other repair-stations—with Red Cross flags flying over them—for the broken men. So in the rear of the sector where the Italians planned to give battle on a front of thirty miles, a series of great base hospitals were established, and, nearer the front, a series of clearing-hospitals, and, still closer up, field-hospitals, and in the immediate rear of the fighting-line, hundreds of dressing-stations and first-aid posts were located in dugouts and bomb-proof shelters. And along the roads stretched endless caravans of gray ambulances, for it promised to be a bloody business. In other words, it was necessary, before the battle could be fought with any hope of success, to build what was to all intents and purposes a great modern city, a city of half a million inhabitants, with many miles of macadamized thoroughfares, with water and telephone and telegraph systems, with a highly efficient sanitary service, with railways, with huge warehouses filled with food and clothing, with more hospitals than any city ever had before, with butcher-shops and bakeries and machine-shops and tailors and boot-menders—in fact, with everything necessary to meet the demands of 500,000 men. Yet Mr.

Bryan and his fellow-members of the Order of the Dove and Olive-Branch would have us believe that all that is necessary in order to win a modern battle is to take the trusty target-rifle from the closet under the stairs, dump a box of cartridges into our pockets, and sally forth, whereupon the enemy, decimated by the deadliness of our fire, will be only too glad to surrender.

The most formidable task which confronted the Italians was that of constructing the vast system of trenches through which the troops could be moved forward in comparative safety to the positions from which would be launched the final assault. This presented no exceptional difficulties in the rich alluvial soil on the Isonzo's western bank, but once the Italians had crossed the river they found themselves on the Carso, through whose solid rock the trenches could be driven only with pneumatic drills and dynamite. All of the Italian trenches that I saw showed a very high skill in engineering. Instead of keeping the earthen walls from crumbling and caving by the use of the wicker-work revetments so general on the Western Front, the Italians use a sort of steel trellis which is easily put in place, and is not readily damaged by shell-fire. Other trenches which I saw (though not on the Carso, of course) were built of solid concrete with steel shields for the riflemen cemented into the parapets.

During these weeks of preparation the Italian aviators, observers, and spies had been busy collecting information concerning the strength of the Gorizia defenses and the disposition of the Austrian batteries and troops. By means of thousands of photographs taken from airplanes, enlarged, and then pieced together, the Italians had as accurate and detailed a map of the Austrian lines of defense as was possessed by the Austrian General Staff itself. Thanks to the data thus obtained, the Italian gunners were able to locate their targets and estimate their ranges with absolute precision. They knew which building in Gorizia was the headquarters of the Austrian commander; they had discovered where his telephone and telegraph stations were located; and they had spotted his observation posts. Indeed, so highly developed was the Italian intelligence service that the Austrians were not able to transfer a battalion or change the position of a battery without the knowledge of General Cadorna.

Now the Austrians, like the newspaper experts, were convinced that the Italians had their hands full in the Trentino without courting trouble on the Isonzo. And if there was to be an attack along the Isonzo front—which they doubted—they believed that it would almost certainly develop in the Monfalcone sector, next the sea. And of this belief the Italians took care not to disabuse them. Here again was exemplified the vital necessity of having control of the air. If, during the latter half of July, the Austrian fliers had been able to get over the Italian lines, they could not have failed to observe the enormous preparations which were in progress, and when the Italians advanced, the Austrians would have been ready for them. But the Italians kept control of the air (during my entire trip on the Italian front I can recall having seen only one Austrian airplane), the Austrians had no means of learning what was impending, and were, therefore, quite unprepared for the attack when it came—and Gorizia fell.

By the 4th of August, 1916, all was ready for the Big Push. On the morning of that day brisk fighting began on the Monfalcone sector. Convinced that this was the danger-point, the Austrian commander rushed his reserves southward to strengthen his threatened line. This was precisely what the Italians wanted. They had succeeded in distracting his attention from their real objective—Gorizia. Now the battle of Gorizia was really not fought at Gorizia at all. What happened was the brilliant and bloody storming of the Austrian positions on Podgora and Monte Sabotino, a simultaneous crossing of the Isonzo opposite Gorizia and at Sagrado, and a splendid rush up to and across the plateau of the Carso which culminated in the taking of Monte San Michele. Gorizia itself was not organized for defense, and so astounded was its garrison at the capture in rapid succession of the city's defending positions, which had been deemed impregnable, that no serious resistance was offered.

On the morning of August 6 a hurricane of steel suddenly broke upon Gorizia. But the Italian gunners had received careful instructions, and instead of blowing the city off the map, as they could easily have done, they confined their efforts to the destruction of the enemy's headquarters, observation posts, and telephone-stations, thus destroying his means of communication and effectually disrupting his entire organization. Other batteries turned their attention to the railway-station, the railway-yards, and the roads, dropping such a curtain of shell-fire behind the town that the Austrians were unable to bring up reinforcements. Care was taken, however, to do as little damage as possible to the city itself, as the Italians wanted it for themselves.

The most difficult, as it was the most spectacular, phase of the attack was the storming of the Sabotino, a mountain two thousand feet high, which, it was generally believed, could never be taken with the bayonet. The Italians, realizing that no troops in the world could hope to reach the summit of those steep slopes in the face of barbed wire, rifles, and machine-guns, had, unknown to the enemy, driven a tunnel, a mile and a quarter long, into the very heart of this position. When the assault was ordered, therefore, the first lines of Italian infantry suddenly appeared from out of the ground within a few yards of the Austrian trenches. Amid a storm of *vivas* the gray wave, with its crest of glistening steel, surged up the few remaining yards of glacis, topped the parapet, and overwhelmed the defenders. Monte Sabotino, the key to the bridge-head and the city, was in the hands of the Italians. But the Austrians intrenched on Hill 240, the highest summit of the

Podgora range, still held out, and it took several hours of savage fighting to dislodge them. This last stronghold taken, the gray-clad infantry suddenly debouched from the sheltering ravines and went swarming down to the Isonzo. Almost simultaneously another division crossed the river several miles below, at Sagrado. Into the stream they went, their rifles held high above their heads, chanting the splendid hymn of Garibaldi. The Austrian shrapnel churned the river into foam, its waters turned from blue to crimson, but the insistent bugles pealed the charge, and the lines of gray swept on. Pausing on the eastern bank only long enough to re-form, the lines again rolled forward. White disks carried high above the heads of the men showed the Italian gunners how far the infantry had advanced and enabled them to gauge their protecting curtain of fire. Though smothered with shells, and swept by machine-guns, nothing could stop them. "Avanti Savoia!" they roared. "Viva! Eviva Italia!"

Meanwhile, under a heavy fire, the Italian engineers were repairing the iron bridge which carried the railway from Milan and Udine across the Isonzo to Gorizia and so to Trieste and Vienna. The great stone bridge over the river had been destroyed the day before beyond the possibility of immediate repair. In an amazingly short time the work was done and the Italian field-batteries went tearing over the bridge at a gallop to unlimber on the opposite bank and send a shower of shrapnel after the retreating Austrians. Close behind the guns poured Carabinieri, Alpini, Bersaglieri, infantry of the line and squadron after squadron of cavalry riding under thickets of lances. A strong force of Carabinieri were the first troops to enter the city, and not until they had taken complete possession and had assumed the reins of the local government, were the line troops permitted to come in.

The fighting continued for three days, the Austrians, though discouraged and to some extent demoralized, making a brave resistance.

In one *dolina* which had been fortified, an officer and a handful of men fought so pluckily against overwhelming odds that, when at length the survivors came out and surrendered, the Italians presented arms to them as a mark of respect and admiration. By the evening of the 9th of August the attack, "one of the most important and violent onslaughts on fortified positions that the European War has yet seen," had been completely successful, and the city of Gorizia, together with the heights that guarded it, including the northern end of the Carso plateau, were in Italian hands. The cost to Italy was 20,000 dead men. It was a high price but, on the other hand, she captured 19,000 prisoners, 67 pieces of artillery, and scores of trench mortars and machine-guns. The moral and strategic results were of incalculable value. The first line of the Austrian defense, deemed one of the strongest on any front, had collapsed beneath the Italian assaults; though the crest of the Carso still remained in Austrian hands, the gateway to Trieste had been opened; and most important of all, the Italian people had gained the self-confidence which they had long lacked and which comes only from military achievement.

In order to reach Gorizia we had to motor for some miles along a road exposed to enemy fire, for the hills dominating the city to the south and east were still in Austrian hands. The danger was minimized as much as possible by screening the roads in the manner I have already described, so, as the officer who accompanied me took pains to explain, if we happened to be hit by a shell, it would be one fired at random. I could see no reason, however, why a random shell wouldn't end my career just as effectually as a shell intended specially for me. Although, thanks to the tunnels of matting, the Austrians cannot see the traffic on the roads, they know that it must cross the bridges, so on them they keep up a continuous rain of projectiles, and there you have to take your chance. The Gorizia bridge-head was not a place where I should have cared to loiter.

It is not a simple matter to obtain permission to visit Gorizia (it is much easier to visit Verdun), for the city is shelled with more or less regularity, and to have visitors about under such conditions is a nuisance. Hence, one cannot get into Gorizia unless bearing a special pass issued by the Comando Supremo. So rigid are the precautions against unauthorized visitors that, though accompanied by two officers of the Staff and travelling in a staff-car, we were halted by the Carabinieri and our papers examined seven times. To this famous force of constabulary has been given the work of policing the occupied regions, and indeed, the entire zone of the armies. With their huge cocked hats, which, since the war began, have been covered with gray linen, their rosy faces, so pink-and-white that they look as though they had been rouged and powdered, and their little upturned waxed mustaches, the Carabinieri always remind me of the gendarmes in comic operas. But the only thing comic about them is their hats. They are the sternest and most uncompromising guardians of the law that I know. You can expostulate with a London bobbie, you can argue with a Paris gendarme, you can on occasion reason mildly with a New York policeman, but not with an Italian carbineer. To give them back talk is to invite immediate and serious trouble. They are supreme in the war zone, for they take orders from no one save their own officers and have the authority to turn back or arrest any one, no matter what his rank. Our chauffeur, who, being attached to the Comando Supremo, had become so accustomed to driving generals and cabinet ministers that he blagued the military sentries, and quite openly sneered at the orders of the Udine police, would jam on his brakes so suddenly that we would almost go through the wind-shield if a carbineer held up his hand.

Gorizia is, or was before the war, a place of some 40,000 inhabitants. It has broad streets, lined by fine white buildings and lovely gardens, and outside the town are excellent medicinal baths. It will, I think, prove a very popular summer resort with the Italians. Though for many months prior to its capture it was within range of the Italian guns, which could have blown it to smithereens, they refrained from doing so because it was desired, if possible, to take the place intact. That, indeed, has been the Italian policy throughout the war: to do as little unnecessary damage as possible. Now the Austrians, who look down on their lost city from the heights to the eastward, refrain from destroying it, as they easily could do, because they cling to the hope that they may get it back again. So, though the bridge-heads are shelled constantly, and though considerable damage has been inflicted on the suburbs, no serious harm has been done to the city itself. By this I do not mean to imply that the Austrians never shell it, for they do, but only in a desultory, half-hearted fashion. During the day that I spent in Gorizia the deserted streets echoed about every five minutes to the screech-bang of an Austrian *arrivé* or the bang-screech of an Italian *départ*.

Finding that the big Hotel du Parc, which is the city's leading hostelry, was closed, we lunched at the more modest Hotel de la Poste. Our luncheon was served us in the kitchen, as, shortly before our arrival, the dining-room had been wrecked by an Austrian shell. Though this had naturally somewhat upset things, we had a really excellent meal: *minestrone,* which, so far as I could discover, is the only variety of soup known to the Italians, mutton, vegetables, a pudding, fruit, the best coffee I have had in Europe since the war began, and a bottle of fine old Austrian wine which, like the German vintages, is no longer procurable in the restaurants of *civilized* Europe. While we ate, there was a brisk exchange of compliments between the Italian and Austrian batteries in progress above the roofs of the town. The table at which we sat was pushed close up against one of the thick masonry columns which supported the kitchen ceiling. It probably would not have been much of a protection had a shell chanced to drop in on us, but it was wonderfully comforting.

I was accompanied on my visit to Gorizia by Signor Ugo Ojetti, the noted Florentine connoisseur who has been charged with the preservation of all the historical monuments and works of art in the war zone. About this charming and cultured genlteman I was told a characteristic story. In the outskirts of Gorizia stands the château of an Austrian nobleman who was the possessor of a famous collection of paintings. Now it is Signor Ojetti's business to save from injury or destruction all works of art which are worth saving, and, after ticketing and cataloguing them, to ship them to a place of safety to be kept until the war is over, when they will be restored to their respective owners. Though the château in question was within the Italian lines, the windows of the ballroom, in which hung the best of the pictures, were within easy range of the Austrian snipers, who, whenever they saw any one moving about inside, would promptly open a brisk rifle fire. Scarcely had Ojetti and his assistant set foot within the room when *ping* came an Austrian bullet through the window, shattering the crystal chandelier over their heads. Then was presented the extraordinary spectacle of the greatest art critic in Italy crawling on hands and knees over a ballroom floor, taking care to keep as close to that floor as possible, and pausing now and then to make a careful scrutiny of the canvases that hung on the walls above him. "That's probably an Allori," he would call to his assistant. "Remember to take that down after it gets dark. The one next to it is good too—looks like a Bordone, though I can't be certain in this light. But don't bother about that picture over the fireplace—it's only a copy and not worth saving. Let the Austrians have it if they want it."

And they told me that through it all he never once lost his dignity or his monocle.

Another interesting figure who joined our little party in Gorizia was a monk who had served as a regimental chaplain since the beginning of the war. He was a broad-shouldered, brown-bearded fellow and, had it not been for the scarlet cross on the breast of his uniform, I should have taken him for a fine type of the Italian fighting man. I rather suspect, though, that when the bugles pealed the signal for the attack, he quite forgot that the wearers of the Red Cross are supposed to be non-combatants. During the Austrian offensive in the Trentino, an Italian army chaplain was awarded the gold medal for valor, the highest military decoration, because he rallied the men of his regiment after all the officers had fallen and led them in the storming of an Austrian position held by a greatly superior force. Another chaplain who had likewise assumed command of officerless troops was awarded the silver medal for valor. As the duties of the army chaplains are supposed to be confined to giving the men spiritual advice, the doubt arose as to whether they were justified in actually fighting, thus risking the loss of their character as non-combatants. This puzzling question was, therefore, submitted to the Pope, who decided that chaplains assuming command of troops who had lost their officers in battle were merely discharging their duty, as they encouraged the men to resist in self-defense. In addition to the regimental chaplains there are, so I was told, thousands of priests and monks serving in the ranks of the Italian armies. Whether, after leading the exciting and adventurous life of a soldier, these men will be content to resume the sandals and the woollen robe, and to go back to the sheltered and monotonous existence of the monastic orders, I very strongly doubt. In any event, their sympathies will have been deepened and their outlook on life immensely broadened.

It rained in torrents during my stay in

Gorizia, but, as we recrossed the Isonzo onto the Friulian plain, the sinking sun burst through a rift in the leaden clouds and turned into a huge block of rosy coral the red rampart of the Carso. Beyond that wall, scarce a dozen miles as the airplane flies, but many times that distance as the big gun travels, lies Trieste. It will be a long road, a hard road, a bloody road which the Italians must follow to attain their City of Desire, and before that journey is ended the red rocks of the Carso will be redder still. But they will finish the journey, I think. For these iron-hard, brown-faced men, remember, are the stuff from which was made those ever-victorious legions that built the Roman Empire—and it is the dream of founding another Empire which is beckoning them on.

V

WITH THE RUSSIANS IN CHAMPAGNE

WHEN the French have been pestered for permission to visit the front by some foreigner—usually an American—until their patience has been exhausted, or when there comes to Paris a visitor to whom, for one reason or another, they wish to show attention, they send him to Rheims. Artists, architects, ex-ambassadors, ex-congressmen, lady journalists, manufacturers in quest of war orders, bankers engaged in floating loans, millionaires who have given or are likely to give money to war-charities, editors of obscure newspapers and monthly magazines, are packed off weekly, in personally conducted parties of a dozen or more, on a day's excursion to the City of the Desecrated Cathedral. They grow properly indignant over the cathedral's shattered beauties, they visit the famous wine-cellars, they hear the occasional crack of a rifle or the crash of a field-gun,* and, upon their return, they write articles for the magazines, and give lectures, and to their friends at home send long letters—usually copied in the local papers—describing their experiences "on the firing-line." "Visiting the front" has, indeed, become as popular a pastime among Americans in Paris as was racing at Longchamps and Auteuil before the war. Hence, no place in the entire theatre of war has had so much advertising as Rheims. No sector of the front has been visited by so many civilians. That is why I am not going to say anything about Rheims—at least about its cathedral. For there is nothing left to say.

Five minutes of brisk walking from the cathedral brings one to the entrance of the famous wine-cellars of Pommery et Cie, the property of the ancient family of de Polignac.

* Since this was written the Germans have bombarded Rheims so heavily, with the evident intention of completing its destruction, that the French military authorities have ordered the evacuation of the civil population.

The space in this underground city is about equally divided between champagne and civilians, for several hundred of the townspeople, who sought refuge here in the opening weeks of the war, still make these gloomy passages their home. As the *caves* have a mean temperature of fifty degrees Fahrenheit they are comfortable enough, and, as they are fifty feet below the surface of the earth, they are safe. So there the more timid citizens live, rent-free, and will continue to live, no doubt, until the end of the war. In normal times, there are shipped from these cellars each day thirty thousand bottles of champagne, and even now, despite the proximity of the Germans—their trenches are only a few hundred yards away—the work of packing and shipping goes on much as usual, though, of course, on a greatly reduced scale, averaging, so I was told, eight thousand bottles daily. By far the greater part of this goes to America, for nowadays Europeans do not buy champagne.

To the red-faced, white-waistcoated, prosperous-looking gentlemen who scan so carefully the hotel wine-lists, I feel sure that it will come as a relief to learn that, though there was no 1916 crop of champagne, the vintages of 1914 and 1915 were exceptionally fine—*grands vins* they will probably be labelled. (And they ought to be, for the vines were watered with the bravest blood of France.) I don't suppose it would particularly interest those same complacent gentlemen, though, were I to add that the price of one of those gilt-topped bottles would keep a French child from cold and hunger for a month.

A few hours before I visited the cellars, a workman, loading cases of champagne in front of the company's offices for export to the United States, was blown to pieces by a German shell. They showed me the shattered columns of the office-building, and on the cobbles of the little square pointed out an ugly stain. So, when I returned to America, and in a famous restaurant, where I was dining, saw white-shirted men and white-shouldered women sipping glasses abrim with the sparkling wine of Rheims, the picture of those bloodstained cobbles in that French city flashed before me, and I experienced a momentary sensation of disgust, for it seemed to me that in the amber depths I caught a stain of crimson. But of course it was only my imagination. Still, I was glad when it came time to leave, for the scene was too suggestive in its contrast to be pleasant: we, in America, eating and drinking and laughing; they, over there in Europe, fighting and suffering and hungering.

Leaving Rheims, we took a great gray car and drove south, ever south, until, as darkness was falling, we reached the headquarters of General Jilinsky, commanding the Russian forces fighting in Champagne. Here the Russians have two infantry brigades, with a total of 16,000 men; there is a third brigade at Salonika. The last time the Russians were in France was in 1814, and then they were there for a different purpose. Little could Napoleon have dreamed that they, who helped to dethrone him, would come back, a century later, as France's allies. Yet this war has produced stranger coincidences than that. The British armies, disembarking at Rouen, tramp through that very square where their ancestors burned the Maid of Orleans. And at Pont des Briques, outside Boulogne, where Napoleon waited impatiently for weeks in the hope of being able to invade England, is now situated the greatest of the British base camps.

General Jilinsky reminded me of a fighting-cock. He is a little man, much the height and build of the late General Funston, with hair cropped close to the skull, after the Russian fashion; through a buttonhole of his green service tunic was drawn the orange-and-black ribbon of the Order of St. George. He can best be described as "a live wire." His staff-officers impressed me as being as efficient and razor-keen as their chief. The general asked me if I would like to visit his trenches, and I assured him that it was the hope of being permitted to do so which had brought me there. Whereupon a staff-officer disappeared into the hall to return a moment later with a gas-mask in a tin case and a steel helmet covered with tan linen.

"You had better take these with you," he said. "There is nearly always something happening on our front, and there is no sense in taking unnecessary risks."

I soon found that the precaution was not an idle one, for, as our car drew up at the entrance to the *boyau* which led by devious windings into the first-line trenches, the group of officers and men assembled in front of brigade headquarters were hastily donning their masks: grotesque-looking contrivances of metal, cloth, and rubber, which in shape resembled a pig's snout.

"Gas," said my Russian companion briefly. "We will stay here until it is over."

Though we must have been nearly a mile behind the firing-line, the air was filled with a sweetish, sickish smell which suggested both the operating-room and the laboratory. So faint and elusive was the odor that I hesitated to follow the example of the others and don my mask, until I remembered having been told at Souchez, on the British front, that a horse had been killed by gas when seven miles behind the lines.

It is a logical development of this use of chemicals as weapons that the horses in use on the French front are now provided with gas-masks in precisely the same manner as the soldiers. These masks, which are kept attached to the harness, ready for instant use, do not cover the entire face, as do those worn by the men, but only the mouth and nostrils. In fact they resemble the feeding-bags which cartmen and cab-drivers put on their horses for the midday meal. Generally speaking, the masks are provided only for artillery horses and those employed in hauling ammunition, though it now seems likely that if the cavalry gets a chance to go into action, masks will be worn by the troopers and their horses alike. After a large gas attack the fumes sometimes settle down in the valleys far behind the lines, and hours may elapse before they are dissipated by the wind. As it not infrequently happens that one of these gas banks settles over a road on which it is imperative that the traffic be not interrupted, large signs are posted notifying all drivers to put the masks on their horses before entering the danger zone.

There are now three different kinds of gases in general use on the Western Front. The best known of these is a form of chlorine gas, which is liberated from cylinders or flasks, to be carried by the wind over the enemy's lines. Contrary to the popular impression, its use is not as general as the newspaper accounts have led the public to believe, for it requires elaborate preparation, can only be employed over comparatively flat ground, and then only when the wind is of exactly the right velocity, neither too light nor too strong. Another form of asphyxiating gas is held in shells in liquid form, usually in lead containers. Upon the bursting of the shell, which is fired from an ordinary field-gun, the liquid rapidly evaporates and liberates the gas, a few inhalations of which are sufficient to cause death. The third type consists of lachrymal, or tear-producing, gas, which is used in the same way as the asphyxiating, but its effects are not fatal, merely putting a man out of action for a few hours. It is really, however, the most efficacious of the three types, as it does not evaporate as readily as the asphyxiating gas. As a well distributed fire of lachrymal shells will form a screen of gas which will last for several hours, they are often used during an attack to prevent the enemy from bringing up reinforcements. Another use is against artillery positions, the clouds of gas from the lachrymal shells making it almost impossible for the men to serve the guns. I was also told of these shells having been used with great success to surround the headquarters of a divisional commander, disabling him and his entire staff during an attack.

Before a change in the wind dissipated the last odors of gas, darkness had fallen. "Now," said my cicerone, "we will resume our trip to the trenches." The last time that I had seen these trenches, which the Russians are now holding, was in October, 1915, during the great French offensive in Champagne, when I had visited them within a few hours after their capture by the French. On that occasion they had been so pounded by the French artillery that they were little more than giant furrows in the chalky soil, and thickly strewn along those furrows was all the horrid garbage of a battlefield: twisted and tangled barbed wire, splintered planks, shattered rifles, broken machine-guns, unexploded hand-grenades, knapsacks, water-bottles, pieces of uniforms, bits of leather, and, most horrible of all, the remains of what had once been human beings. But all this débris had long since been cleared away. Under the skilful hands of the Russians the rebuilt trenches had taken on a neat and orderly appearance. The earthen walls had been revetted with wire chicken-netting, and instead of tramping through ankle-deep mud, we had beneath our feet neat walks of corduroy. We tramped for what seemed interminable miles in the darkness, always zigzagging. Now and then we would come upon little fires, discreetly screened, built at the entrances to dugouts burrowed from the trench-walls. Over these fires soldiers in flat caps and belted greatcoats were cooking their evening meal. I had expected to see unkempt men wearing sheepskin caps, men with flat noses and matted beards, but instead I found clean-shaven, splendidly set-up giants, with the pink skins that come from perfect cleanliness and perfect health. Following the direction of the arrows on signs printed in both French and Russian, we at last reached the fire-trench, where dim figures looking strangely mediæval in their steel helmets, crouched motionless, peering out along their rifle-barrels into the eerie darkness of No Man's Land. Here there was a sporadic illumination, for from the German trenches in front of us lights were rising and falling. They were very beautiful: slender stems of fire arching skyward to burst into blossoms of brilliant sparks, which illuminated the band of shell-pocked soil between the trenches as though it were day. Occasionally there would be a dozen of these star-shells in the air at the same time: they reminded me of the Fourth of July fireworks at Manhattan Beach. In the fire-trenches there is no talking save in whispers, but every now and then the almost uncanny silence would be punctuated by the sharp crack of a rifle, the *tut-tut-tut* of a mitrailleuse, or, from somewhere in the distance, the angry bark of a field-gun.

There was a whispered conversation between the officer in command of the trench and my guide. The latter turned to me.

"We have driven a sap to within thirty metres of the enemy," he said, "and have established a listening-post out there. Would you care to go out to it?"

I would, and said so.

"No talking, then, if you please," he warned me, "and as little noise as possible."

This time the *boyau* was very narrow, and writhed between its earthen walls like a dying snake. We advanced on tiptoe, as cautiously as though stalking big game—as, indeed, we were. Ten minutes of this slow and tortuous progress brought us to the *poste d'écoute*. In a space the size of a hall bedroom half a score of men stood in attitudes of strained expectancy, staring into the blackness through the loopholes in their steel shields. There being no loophole vacant, I took a chance and, standing on the firing step, raised my head above the level of the parapet and made a hurried survey of the few yards of No Man's Land which separated us from the enemy—a space so narrow that I could have thrown a stone across, yet more impassable than the deepest chasm. I was rewarded for the risk by getting a glimpse of a dim maze of wire entanglements, and, just beyond, a darker bulk which I knew for the German trench. And I knew that from that trench sharp eyes were peering out into the darkness toward us just as we were trying to discern them. As I stepped down from my somewhat exposed position a soldier standing a few feet farther along the line raised *his* head above the parapet, as though to relieve his cramped muscles. Just then a star-shell burst above us, turning the trench into day. *Ping!!!* There was a ringing metallic sound, as when a 22-caliber bullet strikes the target in a shooting-gallery, and the big soldier who had incautiously exposed himself crumpled up in the bottom of the trench with a bullet through his helmet and through his brain. The young officer in command of the listening-post cursed softly. "I'm forever warning the men not to expose themselves," he said irritatedly, "but they forget it the next minute. They're nothing but stupid children." He spoke in much the same tone of annoyance he might have used if the man had been a clumsy servant who had broken a valuable dish. Then he went into the tiny dugout where the telephone was, and rang up the trench commander, and asked him to send out a bearer, for the *boyau* communicating with the listening-post was too narrow to admit the passage of a stretcher. The bearer arrived just as we started to return. He was a regular dray-horse of a man, with shoulders as massive and competent as those of a Constantinople *hamel.* Strapped to his back by a sort of harness was a contrivance which looked like a rude armchair with the legs cut off. His comrades hoisted the dead man onto the back of the live man, and with a rope took a few turns about the bodies of both. As we made our slow way back to the fire-trench, and so to the rear, there stumbled at our heels the grunting porter with his ghastly burden. Now and then I would glance over my shoulder and, in the fleeting glare of the star-shells, would glimpse, above the porter's straining shoulders, the head of the dead soldier lolling inertly from side to side, as though very, very tired. . . . And I wondered if in some lonely cabin by the Volga a woman was praying for her boy.

VI

"THEY SHALL NOT PASS!"

GENERAL Gouraud, the one-armed hero of Gallipoli, who commands the forces in Champagne, is the most picturesque and gallant figure in all the armies of France. On my way south I stopped for a night in Chalons-sur-Marne to dine with him. He was living in a comfortable but modest house, evidently the residence of a prosperous tradesman. When I arrived I found the small and rather barely furnished salon filled with officers of the staff, in uniforms of the beautiful horizon blue which is the universal dress of the French army. They were clustered about the marble-topped centre-table, on which, I imagine, the family Bible used to rest, but which now held the steel base of a 380-centimetre shell, which had fallen in a near-by village that afternoon. This monster projectile, as large as the largest of those fired by our coast-defense guns, must have weighed considerably more than a thousand pounds and doubtless cost the Germans at least a thousand dollars, yet all the damage it had done was to destroy a tumble-down and uninhabited cottage, which proves that, save against permanent fortifications, there is a point where the usefulness of these abnormally large guns ceases. While we were discussing this specimen of Bertha Krupp's handicraft, the door opened and General Gouraud entered the room. Seldom have I seen a more striking figure: a tall, slender, graceful man, with a long, brown, spade-shaped beard which did not entirely conceal a mouth both sensitive and firm. But it was the eyes which attracted and held one's attention: great, lustrous eyes, as large and tender as a woman's, but which could on occasion, I fancy, become cold as steel, or angry as lightning. One sleeve of his tunic hung empty, and he leaned heavily on a cane, for during the landing at Gallipoli he was terribly wounded by a Turkish shell.

Covering his breast were glittering stars and crosses, which showed how brilliant had been his services in this and other wars. He is a remarkable man, this soldier with the beard of a *poilu* and the eyes of a poet, and, unless I am greatly mistaken, he is destined to go a long, long way.

It was the sort of dinner that one marks with a white milestone on the road of memory. The soldier-servants wore white-cotton gloves and there were flowers on the table and menus with quaint little military sketches in the corners. General Gouraud talked in his deep, melodious voice of other wars in which he had fought, in Annam and Morocco and Madagascar, and the white-mustached old general of artillery at my left illustrated, with the aid of the knives and forks, a new system of artillery fire, which, he assured me very earnestly, would make pudding of the German trenches. While the salad was being served one of the staff-officers was called to the telephone. When he returned the general raised inquiring eyebrows. *"N'importe, mon général,"* he answered. "Colonel ——— telephoned that the Boches attacked in force south of ———" and he named a certain sector, "but that we have driven them back with heavy losses." Then he resumed his interrupted dinner as unconcernedly as though he had been called to the telephone to be told that the Braves had defeated the Pirates in the ninth inning.

While we were at breakfast the next morning the windows of the hotel dining-room suddenly began to reverberate to the *bang-bang-bang* of guns. Going to the door, we saw, high overhead, a great white bird, which turned to silver when touched by the rays of the morning sun. Though shrapnel bursts were all about it—I counted thirty of the fleecy puffs at one time—it sailed serenely on, a thing of delicate beauty against the cloudless blue. Though few airplanes are brought down by artillery fire, the improvement in anti-aircraft guns has forced the aviators to keep at a height of from 12,000 to 17,000 feet, instead of 2,000, as they did at the beginning of the war. The French gunners have now devised a system which, when it is successfully executed, makes things extremely uncomfortable for the enemy aviator. This system consists in so gauging the fire of the anti-aircraft guns that the airman finds himself in a "box" of shrapnel; that is, one shell is timed to burst directly in front of the machine, another behind it, one above, one below, and one on either side. The dimensions of this "box" of bursting shrapnel are gradually made smaller, so that, unless the aviator recognizes his danger in time, escape becomes impossible, and he is done for. Occasionally an aviator, finding himself caught in such a death-trap, pretends that he has been hit, and lets his machine flutter helplessly earthward, like a wounded bird, until the gunners, believing themselves certain of their prey, cease firing, whereupon the airman skilfully "catches" himself, and, straightening the planes of his machine, goes soaring off to safety. Navarre, one of the most daring of the French fliers, so perfected himself in the execution of this hazardous ruse that he would let go of the controls and permit his machine to literally fall, sometimes from a height of a mile or more, making no attempt at recovery until within sixty metres of the ground, when he would save himself by a hawk-like swoop in which his wheels would actually graze the earth.

The organization of the French air service, with its system of airplane and seaplane squadrons, dirigibles and observation balloons, schools, repair-shops, and manufactories, is entirely an outgrowth of the war. The airplanes are organized in *escadrilles,* usually composed of ten machines each, for three distinct purposes. The bombardment squadrons are made up of slow machines with great carrying capacity, such as the Voisin; the pursuit or battle squadrons—the *escadrilles de chasse*—are composed of small and very fast 'planes, such as the Spad and Nieuport; while the general utility squadrons, used for reconnoissance, artillery regulation, and photographing, usually

"*Halt!* Show Your Papers!"

On the roads in the war zone there are sentries at frequent intervals and they are all suspicious.

A Nieuport Biplane About to Take the Air.

The pursuit or battle squadrons—the *escadrilles de chasse*—are composed of small and very fast planes, such as the Spad and Nieuport.

consist of medium-speed, two-passenger machines like the Farman and the Caudron.

Until very recently the Nieuport biplane, which can attain a speed of one hundred and ten miles an hour, has been considered the fastest and most efficient, as it is the smallest, of the French battle-planes, but it is now outspeeded by the new Spad* machine, which has reached a speed of over one hundred and twenty miles an hour, and of which great hopes are entertained. The Spad, like the Nieuport, is a one-man apparatus, the machine-gun mounted on its upper plane being fired by the pilot with one hand, while with the other hand and his feet he operates his controls. On the "tractors," as the airplanes having the propellers in front are called, the machine-guns are synchronized so as to fire between the whirling blades. Garros, the famous French flier, was the first man to perfect a device for firing a machine-gun through a propeller. He armored the blades so that if struck by a bullet

* A nickname for the Hispana-Suiza.

they would not be injured. This was greatly improved upon by the Germans in the Fokker type, the fire of the machine-guns being automatically regulated so that it is never discharged when a blade of the propeller is directly in front of the muzzle. Since then various forms of this device have been adapted by all the belligerents. Another novel development of aerial warfare is the miniature wireless-sending apparatus with which most of the observation and artillery regulation machines are now equipped, thus enabling the observers to keep in constant touch with the ground. In addition to developing the fastest possible battle-planes, the French are making efforts to build more formidable craft for bombing purposes. The latest of these is a Voisin triplane, which has a total lifting capacity of two tons, carries a crew of five men, and is driven by four propellers, each operated by a 210-horse-power Hispana-Suiza motor. These new motors weigh only about two hundred kilograms, or a little over two pounds per horse-power.

During the past year the French have made most of their raids by nights. One reason for this is that raiding craft, which are comparatively slow machines, are so heavily laden with bombs that they are only able to perform straight flying and hence are easily brought down by the fast and quick-turning battleplanes. Daylight raids, moreover, necessitate an escorting fleet of fighting craft in order to protect the bombing machines, just as a dreadnought has to be protected by a screen of destroyers. Though the dangers of flying are considerably increased by darkness, the French believe this is more than compensated for by the fact that, being comparatively safe from attack by enemy aircraft or from the fire of anti-aircraft guns, the raiders can fly at a much lower altitude and consequently have a much better chance of hitting their targets.

One of the extremely important uses to which airplanes are now put is the destruction of the enemy's observation balloons, on which he depends for the regulation of his artillery fire. An airplane which is to be used for this work is specially fitted with a number of rocket tubes which project in all directions, so that it looks like a pipe-organ gone on a spree. The rockets, which are fired by means of a keyboard not unlike that of a clavier, are loaded with a composition containing a large percentage of phosphorus and are fitted with gangs of barbed hooks. If the rocket hits the balloon these hooks catch in the envelope and hold it there, while the phosphorus bursts into a flame which it is impossible to extinguish. During the fighting before Verdun, eight French aviators, driving machines thus equipped, were ordered to attack eight German balloons. Six of the balloons were destroyed.

But the very last word in aeronautical development is what might be called, for want of a better term, an aerial submarine. I refer to seaplanes carrying in clips beneath the fuselage specially constructed 18-inch torpedoes. In the under side of this type of torpedo is an opening. When the torpedo is dropped into the sea the water, pouring into this opening, sets the propelling mechanism in motion and the projectile goes tearing away on its errand of destruction precisely as though fired from the torpedo-tube of a submarine. It may be recalled that some months ago the papers printed an account of a Turkish transport, loaded with soldiers, having been torpedoed in the Sea of Marmora, the accepted explanation being that a submarine had succeeded in making its way through the Dardanelles. As a matter of fact, that transport was sunk by a torpedo dropped from the air! The pilot of a Short seaplane had winged his way over the Gallipoli Peninsula, had sighted the troop-laden transport steaming across the Marmora Sea, and, volplaning down until he was only twenty-five feet above the water and a few hundred yards from the doomed vessel, had jerked the lever which released the torpedo. As it struck the water its machinery was automatically set going, something that looked like a giant cigar went streaking through the waves

. . . there was a shattering explosion, and when the smoke cleared away the transport had disappeared. Whereupon the airman, his mission accomplished, flew back to his base in the Ægean. There may be stranger developments of the war than that, but if so I have not heard of them.

France is now (April, 1917) turning out between eight hundred and a thousand completely equipped airplanes a month, but a considerable proportion of these are for the use of her allies. I have asked many persons who ought to know how many airplanes France has in commission, and, though the replies varied considerably, I should say that she has at present somewhere between five thousand and seven thousand machines in or ready to take the air.*

Leaving Chalons in the gray dawn of a winter's morn, we fled southward again, through

* Though great numbers of American-built airplanes have been shipped to Europe, they are being used only for purposes of instruction, as they are not considered fast enough for work on the front.

Bar-le-Duc (the place, you know, where the jelly comes from) the words *"Caves voutés"* chalked on the doors of those buildings having vaulted cellars showing that air raids were of frequent occurrence, and so, through steadily increasing traffic, to Souilly, the obscure hamlet from which was directed the defense of Verdun. In the centre of the cobble-paved Grande Place stood the Mairie, a two-story building in the uncompromising style characteristic of most French provincial architecture. At the foot of the steps stood two sentries in mud-caked uniforms and dented helmets, and through the front door flowed an endless stream of staff-officers, orderlies, messengers, and mud-spattered despatch riders. In this village *mairie,* a score of miles behind the firing-line, were centred the nerve and vascular systems of an army of half a million men; here was planned and directed the greatest battle of all time. On the upper floor, in a large, light, scantily furnished room, a man with a great silver star on the breast of his light-blue tunic sat at a table, bent over a map. He had rather sparse gray hair and a gray mustache and a little tuft of gray below the lower lip. His eyes were sunken and tired-looking, as though from lack of sleep, and his face and forehead were deeply lined, but he gave the impression, nevertheless, of possessing immense vitality and energy. He was a broad-shouldered, solidly built, four-square sort of man, with cool, level eyes, and a quiet, almost taciturn manner. It was General Robert Nivelle, the man who held Verdun for France. He it was who, when the fortress was quivering beneath the Germans' sledge-hammer blows, had quietly remarked: "They shall not pass!" *And they did not.*

I did not remain long with General Nivelle; to have taken much of such a man's time would have been a rank impertinence. I would go to Verdun? he inquired. Yes, with his permission, I answered. Everything had been arranged, he assured me. An officer who knew America well—Commandant Bunau-Varilla, of Panama Canal fame—had been assigned to go with me.* As I was leaving I attempted to express to him the admiration which I felt for the fashion in which he had conducted the Great Defense. But with a gesture he waved the compliment aside. "It is the men out there in the trenches who should be thanked," he said. "They are the ones who are holding Verdun." I took away with me the impression of a man as stanch, as confident, as unconquerable as the city he had so heroically defended. A few weeks later he was to succeed Marshal Joffre to the highest field command in the gift of the French Government.

It is twenty miles from Souilly to Verdun, and the road has come to be known as La Voie Sacré—the Sacred Way—because on the uninterrupted flow of ammunition and supplies over that road depended the safety of the fortress. Three thousand men with picks and shovels, working day and night, kept the road

* Commandant Bunau-Varilla was really sent as a compliment to my companion, Mr. Arthur Page, editor of *The World's Work*.

in condition to bear up under the enormous volume of traffic. The railway to Verdun was so repeatedly cut by German shells that the French built a narrow-gauge line, which zigzags over the hills. Beside the road, at frequent intervals, I noted cisterns and watering-troughs, and huge overhead water-tanks; for an army—men, horses, and motor-cars—is incredibly thirsty. This elaborate water system is the work of Major Bunau-Varilla, who, fittingly enough, is the head of the *Service d'Eau des Armées.*

Half a dozen miles out of Souilly we crossed the watershed between the Seine and the Rhine and were in the valley of the Meuse. On the other side of yonder hill, whence came a constant muttering of cannon, was, I knew, the Unconquerable City.

While yet Verdun itself was out of sight, we came, quite unexpectedly, upon one of its mightiest defenders: a 400-millimetre gun mounted on a railway-truck. So streaked and striped and splashed and mottled with many colors was it that, monster though it was, it escaped my notice until we were almost upon it. Suddenly a score or more of grimy men, its crew, came pelting down the track, as subway laborers run for shelter when a blast is about to be set off. A moment later came a mighty bellow; from the up-turned nose of the monster burst a puff of smoke pierced by a tongue of flame, and an invisible express-train went roaring eastward in the direction of the German lines. This was the mighty weapon of which I had heard rumors but had never seen: the great 16-inch howitzer with which the French had so pounded Fort Douaumont as to cause its evacuation by the Germans.

The French artillerists were such firm believers in the superiority of light over heavy artillery, and pinned such faith to their 75's, that they had paid scant attention to the question of heavy mobile guns. Hence when the German tidal wave rolled Parisward in 1914, the only heavy artillery possessed by the

French consisted of a very few 4.2-inch Creusot guns of a model adopted just prior to the war, and a limited number of batteries of 4.8-inch and 6.1-inch guns and howitzers; all of them, save only the 6.1-inch Rimailho howitzer of 1904, being models twenty to forty years old. These pieces were, of course, vastly outclassed in range and smashing power by the heavy guns of the Central Powers, such as the German 420's (the famous "42's") and the Austrian 380's. Undismayed, however, the French set energetically to work to make up their deficiencies. As it takes time to manufacture guns, large numbers of naval pieces were pressed into service, most of them being mounted on railway-trucks, thus insuring extreme mobility. The German 42's, I might mention in passing, lack this very essential quality, as they can be fired only from specially built concrete bases, from which they cannot readily be moved. The two German 42's which pounded to pieces the barrier forts of Antwerp were mounted on concrete platforms

Verdun's Mightiest Defender: a 400-mm. Gun.

This was the great 16-inch weapon with which the French so pounded Fort Douaumont as to cause its evacuation by the Germans.

A Gun Painted to Escape the Observation of Enemy Airmen.

"So streaked and striped and splashed and mottled with many colors was it that, monster though it was, it escaped my notice until we were almost upon it."

behind a railway embankment near Malines, where they remained throughout the siege of the city.

Some idea may be had of the variety of artillery in use on the French front when I mention that there are at least eleven calibers of guns, howitzers, and mortars, ranging in size from 9 inches to 20.8 inches, in action between Switzerland and the Somme. All of these, with a very few exceptions, are mounted on railway-trucks. In fact, the only large calibered piece not thus mounted is the Schneider mortar, a very efficient weapon, having a remarkably smooth recoil, which has a range of over six miles. It is transported, with its carriage and platform, in six loads, each weighing from four to five tons, about four hours being required to set up the piece ready for firing. Nearly all of these railway guns are, I understand, naval or coast-defense pieces, some of them being long-range weapons cut down to form howitzers or mortars, while others have been created by boring to a larger caliber a gun whose rifling had been worn out in use. For example, the 400-millimetre, already referred to as having proved so effective against Douaumont, was, I am told, made by cutting down and boring out a 13.6-inch naval gun. But the master gun, the very latest product of French brains and French foundries, is the huge 520-millimetre (20.8-inch) howitzer which has just been completed at the Schneider works at Creusot. This, the largest gun in existence, has a length of 16 calibers (that is, sixteen times its bore, or approximately 28 feet), and weighs 60 tons. It fires a shell 7 feet long, weighing nearly 3,000 pounds, and carrying a bursting charge of 660 pounds of high explosive. Its range is 18 kilometres, or a little over eleven miles, though this can probably be increased if desired. This is France's answer to the German 42's, and, just as the latter shattered the forts of Liége, Antwerp, and Namur, so these new French titans will, it is confidently believed, humble the pride of Metz and Strasbourg.

So insistent has been the demand from the front for big guns, and yet more big guns, that new batteries are being formed every day. Generally speaking, the French plan is to assign short-range howitzers and mortars to the division; the longer range, horse-drawn guns —*hippomobile* the French designate them—to the army corps; while the tractor-drawn pieces and those mounted on railway-carriages are placed directly under the orders of the chief of artillery of each army.

A new, and in many respects one of the most effective weapons produced by the war is the trench mortar. These light and mobile weapons, of which the French have at least four calibers, ranging from 58-millimetres to 340-millimetres, are under the direction of the artillery, and should not be confused with the various types of bomb-throwers, which are operated by the infantry. The latest development in trench weapons is the Van Deuren mortar, which takes its name from the Belgian officer who is its inventor. Its chief peculiarity lies in the fact that its barrel consists of a solid core instead of a hollow tube like all other guns. Attached to the base of the shell is a hollow winged shaft which fits over the core of the gun, the desired range being obtained by varying the length of the powder-chamber: that is, the distance between the end of the barrel and the base of the shell proper. The gun is fired at a fixed elevation, and is so small and light that it can readily be moved and set up by a couple of men in a few minutes. In no branch of the artillery has such advancement been made as in the trench mortars, which have now attained almost as great a degree of accuracy as the field-gun. Such great importance is attached to the trench mortars by the Italians that they have formed them into a distinct arm of the service, entirely independent of the artillery, the officers of the trench-mortar batteries, who are drawn from the cavalry, being trained at a special school.

The city of Verdun, or rather the blackened ruins which are all that remain of it, stands in the centre of a great valley which is shaped not unlike a platter. Down this valley, splitting the city in half, meanders the River Meuse. The houses of Verdun, like those of so many mediæval cities, are clustered about the foot of a great fortified rock. From this rock Vauban, at the order of Louis XIV, blasted ramparts and battlements. To meet the constantly changing conditions of warfare, later generations of engineers gradually honeycombed the rock with passages, tunnels, magazines, store-rooms, halls, and casemates, a veritable labyrinth of them, thus creating the present Citadel of Verdun. Then, because the city and its citadel lie in the middle of a valley dominated by hills—like a lump of sugar in the middle of a platter—upon those hills was built a chain of barrier forts: La Chaume, Tavannes, Thiaumont, Vaux, Douaumont, and others. But when, at Liége and Namur, at Antwerp and Maubeuge, the Germans proved conclusively that no forts could long withstand the battering of their heavy guns, the French took instant profit by the lesson. They promptly left the citadel and the forts nearest to it and established themselves in trenches on the surrounding hills, taking with them their artillery. This trench-line ran through certain of the small outlying forts, such as Tavannes, Thiaumont, Douaumont, and Vaux, and that is why you have read in the papers so much of the desperate fighting about them. Thus the much-talked-of fortress of Verdun was no longer a fortress at all, but merely a sector in that battle-line which extends from the Channel to the Alps. Barring its historic associations, and the moral effect which its fall might have in France and abroad, its capture by the Germans would have had no more strategic importance, if as much, than if the French line had been bent back for a few miles at Rheims, or Soissons, or Thann. The Vauban citadel in the city became merely an advanced headquarters, a telephone exchange, a supply station, a sort of central office, from the safety of whose subterranean casemates General Dubois, the commander of the city, directed the execution of the orders which he received from General Nivelle at Souilly, twenty miles away. Though the citadel's massive walls have resisted the terrific bombardments to which it has been subjected, it has neither guns nor garrison: they are far out on the trench-line beyond the encircling hills. It has, in fact, precisely the same relation to the defense of the Verdun sector that Governor's Island has to the defense of New York. This it is important that you should keep in mind. It should also be remembered that Verdun was held not for strategic but for political and sentimental reasons. The French military chiefs, as soon as they learned of the impending German offensive, favored the evacuation of the city, whose defense, they argued, would necessitate the sacrifice of thousands of lives without any corresponding strategic benefit. But the heads of the Government in Paris looked at things from a different point of view. They realized that, no matter how negligible was its military value, the people of other countries, and, indeed, the French people themselves, believed that Verdun *was* a great fortress; they knew that its capture by the Germans would be interpreted by the world as a French disaster and that the morale of the French people, and French prestige abroad, would suffer accordingly. So, at the eleventh hour and fifty-ninth minute, when the preparations for evacuating the city were all but complete, imperative word was flashed from Paris that it must be held. And it was. Costly though the defense has been, the result has justified it. The Crown Prince lost what little military reputation he possessed—if he had any to lose; his armies lost 600,000 men in dead and wounded; and the world was shown that German guns and German bayonets, no matter how overwhelming in number, cannot break down the steel walls of France.

It was my great good fortune, when the fate of Verdun still hung in the balance, to visit the city and to lunch with General Dubois